1/00

3000 800052 53493
St. Louis Community College

D0847816

 St. Louis Community College

Forest Park
Florissant Valley
Meramec

Instructional Resources
St. Louis, Missouri

INSIDE
OUTSIDE

BETWEEN ARCHITECTURE AND LANDSCAPE

GLOUCESTER MASSACHUSETTS

ROCKPORT PUBLISHERS

Anita Berrizbeitia and Linda Pollak

Copyright © 1999 by Rockport Publishers, Inc.

All rights reserved. No part of this book may be reproduced in any form without written permission of the copyright owners. All images in this book have been reproduced with the knowledge and prior consent of the artists concerned and no responsibility is accepted by producer, publisher, or printer for any infringement of copyright or otherwise, arising from the contents of this publication. Every effort has been made to ensure that credits accurately comply with information supplied.

First published in the United States of America by
Rockport Publishers, Inc.
33 Commercial Street
Gloucester, Massachusetts 01930-5089
Telephone: (978) 282-9590
Facsimile: (978) 283-2742

Distributed to the book trade and art trade in the United States by
North Light Books, an imprint of
F & W Publications
1507 Dana Avenue
Cincinnati, Ohio 45207
Telephone: (800) 289-0963

Other distribution by
Rockport Publishers, Inc.
Gloucester, Massachusetts 01930-5089

ISBN 1-56496-631-3

10 9 8 7 6 5 4 3 2 1

Designer: Stoltze Design
Cover image: Frontcover
        School at Morella, Morella, Spain, Carmen Pinós and Enric Miralles, Architects
        Backcover
        Top left: Villa Dall'Ava, St. Cloud, France, Rem Koolhaas, Architect
        Top right: Etienne Dolet Public Housing, Issy-les Molineaux, France, Catherine Mosbach, Architect
        Bottom left: Municipal Ocean Swimming pool, Leça de Palmeira, Matushinos, Portugal, Alvaro Siza, Architect
        Bottom right: Querini Stampalia Foundation, Venice, Italy, Carlo Scarpa, Architect

Printed in China

INSIDE

BETWEEN ARCHITECTURE AND LANDSCAPE

OUTSIDE

St. Louis Community College
at Meramec
LIBRARY

ROCKPORT

for Sandro and Andrea
and for Luis Daniel, Guillermo, Gustavo, and Luis Daniel

We would like to thank the architects, landscape architects, artists, and their associates, whose work contributes so significantly to this book. In addition we are indebted to our research assistants, Edie Drcar, Gwynne Keathley, Kate Orff, and especially Richard Griswold, who was the production coordinator for the first phase of this project. We also want to acknowledge those people who have helped us with their critique and comments along the way, including Sandro Marpillero, Mathew Becker and Don Freeman. Special thanks to the Harvard Graduate School of Design, in particular to Dean Peter Rowe, and to the departments of architecture and landscape architecture, as well as Associate Dean Russell Sanna, all of whom have supported our research in multiple ways. We also add our warmest thanks to Beth Meyer for her insightful foreword, to Mark Denton for his thoughtful and attentive editing, as well as to Winnie Prentiss and Silke Braun of Rockport Publishers, all of whom have contributed to the production of this book.

Anita Berrizbeitia and Linda Pollak

Contents

FOREWORD
Elizabeth Meyer   9

**OPERATIONS BETWEEN ARCHITECTURE
AND LANDSCAPE**   10

I. RECIPROCITY   14
  Querini Stampalia Foundation   16
  Carlo Scarpa

  Loyola Law School   22
  Frank O. Gehry & Associates, Inc.

  Villa Dall' Ava   28
  Rem Koolhaas, Office for Metropolitan Architecture

  School at Morella   36
  Carmen Pinós & Enric Miralles

  Barnes Residence   42
  Patkau Architects

II. MATERIALITY   48
  Brion Cemetery   50
  Carlo Scarpa

  Stone House   56
  Herzog & De Meuron

  Bamboo Garden   62
  Alexandre Chemetoff, Bureau des Paysages

  Igualada Cemetery   68
  Enric Miralles & Carmen Pinós

  Thomson Factory   76
  Desvigne and Dalnoky

III. THRESHOLD 82

Kimbell Art Museum 84
Louis Kahn

Municipal Ocean Swimming Pool 90
Alvaro Siza

Haarlemmer Houttuinen Housing 98
Herman Hertzberger

Villa Cecilia 104
Torres and Lapeña

Etienne Dolet Public Housing 112
Catherine Mosbach

Robert F. Wagner, Jr. Park 120
Machado Silvetti Associates, Inc.
Olin Partnership

IV. INSERTION 126

Plaça del General Moragues 128
Olga Tarrasó

Fossar de les Moreres 134
Carmen Fiol

Two-way Mirror Cylinder Inside Cube and Video Café 140
Dan Graham
Baratloo-Balch Architects

Jacob Javits Plaza 146
Martha Schwartz, Inc.

V. INFRASTRUCTURE 152

Tunnel-Footbridge 154
Georges Descombes

Wind Screen 160
Maarten Struijs

Plaça de les Glories Catalanes 166
Andreu Arriola

Allegheny Riverfront Park 174
Michael Van Valkenburgh Associates, Inc.

REFERENCES 182

PROJECT CREDITS 186

PHOTO CREDITS 188

ABOUT THE AUTHORS 191

Foreword

This book discusses twenty-four recent design projects, from seven countries, which explore the territory between architecture and landscape. It proposes five strategies, or operations, that characterize these projects. But most important, this book written by two talented designers and educators demonstrates how to reinvigorate our descriptive vocabulary and analytical terms. *Inside Outside* is about how to see anew, and how to reconceptualize interconnections between landscape and architecture. As such, it maps out several alternatives to trite terms—man-versus-nature, formal to informal, hardscape and softscape—that permeate discussion and description of architecture and landscape. As these impoverished discourses continue to limit design possibilities and, perhaps more disconcertingly, limit our experience of living in the world between inside and outside, Berrizbeitia and Pollak provide both a powerful critique of prevailing tendencies and an admirable example for future criticism and design.

This is what differentiates their work from so many other recent publications. Over the past decade, dozens of anthologies about the contemporary designed landscape have been published. Few offer a critical lens for comparing, or even understanding, design vocabulary and operations. Most are loosely edited collections of various designers' images and descriptions of their work. Publications on architecture have, admittedly, a better record of critical assessment. But their discussions about the landscape are too frequently restricted by a rhetoric of architectural hierarchy and dominance over landscape.

How does *Inside Outside* overcome these problems? First, Berrizbeitia and Pollak develop two conceptual frameworks that undergird their twenty-four essays. Eschewing the formal description of elements or objects, they formulate a theory of relationships around the concept of *operations*. Berrizbeitia's and Pollak's theorizing of the exchanges between the domains of the interior and exterior creates a space for the actions of the designer in a variety of places, and at a number of scales: theoretically, as the designer encroaches on the boundaries of her/his discipline; during the design process, conceptually exploring strategies and operations through models or drawings; later, while detailing seams and joints between territories and materials; and on-site during construction, when the interconnections between a design proposition and the existing landscape are negotiated in inches and mediated with tangible substances.

Secondly, the twenty-four disparate projects are related to one another by a common approach evident in each of the essays. The concept of operations, of how designed elements work on one another, is revealed through writing that itself unfolds—immersing readers in their relationship to a place experienced, through movement, over time. By locating the act of knowing in engagement, and not detachment, Berrizbeitia and Pollak provide a theory of landscape and architectural operations that can extend from the act of design to the act of perception. Ideas and interconnections imagined in the studio and constructed on-site are reenacted with each visit, each passage, each encounter between humans and a designed project.

Elizabeth Meyer
Associate Professor, Department of Landscape Architecture
University of Virginia School of Architecture
Charlottesville, Virginia

Operations between architecture and landscape

This book constructs a framework of interpretation for architecture and landscape in order to disclose relationships between them that are often overlooked. Notwithstanding the fact that architecture and landscape inhabit each other's conceptual and physical space, a combination of factors has fostered a deep and enduring division between them. This division has not only impoverished both discourses, it has had a negative impact on the built environment.

The disciplinary and professional boundaries of architecture and landscape architecture have conditioned the perception of what is possible within a project, upholding the Enlightenment idea that each discipline represents a consolidated and exclusive territory of concerns. Recent manifestations of the schism between the disciplines include, on the one side, architecture's agenda of recovering its formal autonomy, and on the other, landscape architecture's ecological focus and disinterest in artistic self-consciousness. Academic curricula and professional practice participate in maintaining this mutual exclusion. The allocation of contracts involving professional collaborations, and even the scheduling of tasks within a project such that design occurs sequentially rather than simultaneously, all impede opportunities for significant collaboration, often resulting in isolated efforts and disjointed built environments.

Our study of relationships between architecture and landscape hinges on a notion of interdisciplinarity (Bhaba, 1990) that goes beyond the reunion of contents, contexts or formal languages within a project, which would merely augment the positivity of existing conventions. It is, instead, a bringing together of modes of thought, with the recognition that each time a practice is transferred across disciplines it is different. That is, it not only generates differences within the other discipline, but also becomes different itself, as a practice. The incorporation of practices of architecture and landscape architecture is understood dynamically, as they are brought into new disciplinary contexts. Therefore, while it is not possible or even desirable to erase disciplinary boundaries, this book momentarily suspends them in order to bring forth different kinds of knowledge. At times, this knowledge might escape the terms of building and landscape altogether, focusing on how elements share an urban space, an ecosystem, or a temporal frame.

The exploration of the territory between architecture and landscape reveals how relationships that transgress disciplinary boundaries can contribute to the definition and enrichment of a discipline. This in-between territory also engages each discipline's expanded field of relationships, including other disciplines such as urban design and ecology. Thus, a building project might engage topographical concerns that would once have been assumed to be part of landscape architecture; or landscape might affect orders of an interior, typically thought of as within the domain of architecture. Yet projects cannot endlessly enlarge their scope of concerns and still maintain their power or integrity. A successful project constructs relationships in precise ways to produce a new set of concerns, with its own set of parameters.

This book is structured according to five *operations*, each of which articulates a conceptual approach to relations between architecture and landscape. An operation is a "procedure or process of a technical nature" that constructs a specific mode of relation between elements. We have adapted Rosalind Krauss' and Yves-Alain Bois' framing of the concept of operation from their exhibition *L'informe: Mode d'emploi* at the Pompidou Center in 1996 (Sedofsky, 1996; Krauss and Bois, 1998). Its emphasis on action supports a potential for significance to be found in the activity of relating.

The notion of operation undermines the autonomy of the individual disciplines of architecture and landscape architecture. Its objective is to conceptualize things that are different from each other—beginning with architecture and landscape—through specific frameworks and with specific terms that are not the sole province of either, and that therefore must be invented for both.

The five operations explored here—reciprocity, materiality, threshold, insertion, and infrastructure—each challenge disciplinary precepts that have served to maintain a rigid dichotomy between architecture and landscape architecture. Thus, reciprocity stands against hierarchy, an ordering principle through which architecture has historically subjugated landscape; materiality challenges an aesthetic tradition of disembodied contemplation; threshold precludes a fixed and static conception of boundary; insertion calls into question a figure/ground formulation of the city; and infrastructure critiques an assumption of landscape as originary ground. Each operation functions at several levels within a project, including its practical activity—the "nuts and bolts"—and also becoming its representational content: for instance, both constructing and representing reciprocity.

The five operations are not static, preexisting categories that a project must fit, nor do they prescribe particular criteria that projects need to fulfill. They become legible and acquire substance through the interpretation of projects, each of which builds a small piece of their conceptual framework. This lack of fixed identity allows the framework to resist becoming an instrument of classification, and to maintain its focus on the relationships between elements rather than on the elements themselves. The operations support an interpretation of architecture and landscape architecture in terms of particular, active relationships—the "how" rather than the "what" of a project—rather than by fixing an aspect of either architecture or landscape's supposedly intrinsic identity.

The exploratory nature of this inquiry precludes describing design work in the context of either discipline's conventional framework. As "transitional thinking," it sometimes requires the invention of language (Flax, 1990). For instance, each of the words that is the title of one of the five operations is slightly displaced from its traditional meaning, in order to do an unfamiliar job, that is, to imply active construction of particular relationships. While all five operations define a condition, reciprocity, insertion, and materiality also suggest a possible action, because they exist in the form of verbs as well as nouns. We use all five terms as if they possessed this dual sense. That the terms threshold and infrastructure exist (in English) only as nouns is offset by the fact that they represent unique conditions of spatial and material interaction.

The operation of reciprocity subverts the hierarchy embedded in the historical dichotomy between architecture and landscape, which has construed landscape as merely the ground on which architecture rests. It recognizes the identity of both landscape and architecture as constructed. This formulation challenges the architectural paradigm of the machine in the garden—

a vision that opposes architecture's progressive alliance with technology to a nostalgic formulation of landscape as timeless and untouched nature.

The operation of materiality critiques the conception of landscape and architecture in purely visual terms by focusing on how both practices explicitly share the operation of reconfiguring matter. It challenges the way in which a classical aesthetic framework has relegated matter to the service of form. The ideas and innovations that contribute to this operation come as often from agricultural traditions and art practices as from design.

The three remaining sections look at urban spaces that include nature, in an attempt to reconceptualize relations between architecture, landscape, and city. This reconceptualization challenges the present-day relevance of the nineteenth-century pastoral park—an artificially recreated naturalistic landscape derived from the English landscape garden. Often occupying vast tracts of land, parks were conceived as an antidote to the congested conditions of city life. While American parks continue to be perceived and designed through this model, it has been increasingly trivialized, both by the reduction in the size of parks, and by the failure to acknowledge complex cultural changes. Contemporary theorists agree that significant innovation will come from changing the way we design public space, not only by developing alternative models, but also by reframing notions such as "nature" and "public" in ways that are relevant to present-day built environments (Muschamp et al., 1993).

The operation of threshold explicitly rejects the reduction of passage to an abrupt crossing of a thin edge, or the gratuitous continuity between two entities. Rather, threshold is understood as a place of becoming, from which identity as well as relationships can emerge. This proposition links a challenge to the autonomy of architecture and landscape with a challenge to autonomy as a necessary precondition of identity in general. It enables a conscious privileging of the spatial and material condition of "between." It is less about the actual physical permeability of this in-between realm, and more about its role in the formation of identity.

The operation of insertion sets up activities of relating between a space and its surroundings. Each project in this section is part of an urban continuum, but also represents a break in that continuum—a break that allows the project to exist as a positive entity in its own right, rather than becoming subsumed within a larger whole. This formulation challenges a figure/ground conception of the city, in which "open" space is often merely that which is left over around building-objects. Configuring the boundaries of a space in order to support communication between spaces is a critical aspect of this operation, to define a place apart from the city that can also form and contribute to its surroundings.

Finally, the operation of infrastructure posits both architecture and landscape as originary conditions in an urban environment, where a "natural" or "true" or "real" ground no longer exists. This formulation challenges the idea of a seamless surface—specifically the ubiquitous undulating lawn of the modern landscape—that blurs particularities and differences. Ever since this paradigm emerged in the late eighteenth century, with the work of Lancelot "Capability" Brown, an obsession with it "seems to have prevented theory from addressing the many other types of site that the modern world has called for . . . ."(Hunt, 1992). In infrastructure, the graft that joins landscape to architecture remains visible in an unselfconscious manner, challenging a naturalistic conception of landscape whose "art" is dedicated to concealment.

Each of the five operations initiates an alternative way of looking. Each one leads in a different direction, away from the circumscribed territories of disciplines in order to articulate and make visible underconceptualized aspects of design. They present opportunities for design outside the scope of conventional discourse, and provide an alternative approach to the construction and representation of relationships between architecture, landscape, city, and subject.

The criteria for selection of the twenty-four projects was that each one function as a vehicle for the exploration of an operation. Each project contributes to the definition of that operation by representing a particular aspect of it. In this way, the four or five projects together yield a broad understanding. While the selection of projects was not guided by typological considerations, differences that emerged between the project groups in terms of sponsorship, scale, and use suggest that a next step—beyond the scope of this book—would be to consider the intersection of each operation with social, political, and economic issues.

The texts that accompany the projects are neither factual description nor personal impressions, but rather speculation to substantiate an operation. The effort throughout has been to insist on relationships between things—whether disciplines or artifacts—rather than on things in themselves. Particular modes of description, including captions that emphasize the position from which something is seen, encourage a reader's awareness of spatial characteristics, as opposed to focusing on how things look.

This book has been a collaborative project. As an architect and a landscape architect, we bring to it a common desire to explore the area between the boundaries of our disciplines. We recognize, however, that we are the product of these disciplines, as well as our individual histories, and that, because our starting points differ, so do our trajectories. The texture of this book reflects these differences, as well as our capacity to respond to each other's insights, which has grown during the writing process.

RECIPROCITY

This section examines how the operation of reciprocity diminishes physical and conceptual separations between architecture and landscape, as well as the traditional hierarchies that privilege one over the other. In the projects presented here, neither order emerges as dominant: even when the origin of a project's development resides in architecture or landscape architecture, the other does not become a passive recipient of that original order.

This interpretation of reciprocity is not about formal gestures that "tie together" outside and inside. Instead, it is dependent on structural relations that often begin with one or more large-scale decisions that forecast and support more visibly apparent local strategies. This is the case with the restructuring of the circulation inside the Palazzo Querini, to engage the canal within its interior, with the breaking down of the perimeter of the Morella school precinct in order to relate the scale of the buildings to that of the site, and with the substitution of a campus arrangement for a single building commission at the Loyola Law School.

The combination of multiple strategies at different scales—for instance, a formal strategy at one scale with a site-specific one at another scale—supports a reciprocal relationship between architecture and landscape that is less dependent on form, and more particular to the contingencies of program and site. An example of this multivalence can be found at Loyola, where strategies belonging to both architecture and landscape support two kinds of inversions, which are complemented by the introduction of intermediate elements.

In most cases, the siting of a building disrupts a landscape. This disruption offers the opportunity for architecture to be an agent of the physical and conceptual reconstruction of the environment it has disrupted, and, in doing so, to establish a reciprocal relationship with it. One strategy of reconstruction involves the physical and visual internalization of the topography of the surrounding landscape. Such is the case of the Barnes Residence, the Villa Dall'Ava, and the School at Morella: In each, the interior of the building becomes part of the surrounding landscape, and also represents that landscape. The topography of the landscape thus becomes the conceptual as well as the physical content of the architecture.

A second reconstructive strategy applies a principle of landscape structure to the design of a building interior. In the Barnes Residence, for instance, the implementation of

a principle of heterogeneity, derived from landscape ecology, produces an unevenness of interior space more typically associated with the spatial structure of a landscape. As in a biological process of cross-fertilization, the introduction of the "weaker" species of landscape breaks down architecture's dominance from within.

Ambiguity can also support reciprocity, by assigning an equivalent status to things, through a strategy that renders their identity uncertain, thereby opening up possibilities for the user's individual interpretation. This kind of ambiguity is found at the Morella School, where the architects manipulate the figure/ground relationship in order to emphasize in-between spaces such as terraces, ramps, and gardens that are conventionally rendered as voids. Heightening this ambiguity at Morella is the alteration of a subject's spatial perceptions, accomplished by the manipulation of his or her bodily position in relation to the landscape. Exterior spaces are made to feel sheltered, as if they were interior spaces; and interior spaces are made to feel exposed and vulnerable, as if isolated in an open landscape.

Another strategy that supports reciprocity is the conceptualization of one thing as its traditional opposite. For example, in the Querini Stampalia Foundation, Scarpa conceptualizes the palazzo interior as an exterior, by creating a landscape of water control structures within it. This landscape also operates as an apparatus that measures natural phenomena, revealing the interior of the building to be as unpredictable and dynamic as the environment outside.

Reciprocity often depends on architecture that is made up of, or broken down into, multiple elements. This combination of fragmentation and multiplicity serves to open the architectural work in such a way as to be able to engage the landscape not as opposite but as elements of connection and use, similar in kind to elements of architecture.

In all of the projects in this section, reciprocity is an active and ongoing condition, in which the exchange between architecture and landscape creates something further and unpredictable, that cannot be contained within the origin of the work. Each project establishes specific terms according to which it produces orders of architecture-landscape that sustain new identities as they redefine their origins.

QUERINI STAMPALIA FOUNDATION

Renovation of the ground floor and garden
Venice, Italy
1959–1963
Carlo Scarpa, Architect

(above) View from bridge toward palazzo.
Watergates are to the left of the bridge.

(below) Main exhibition hall, previously the
androne, looking from the causeway toward the
garden. Glass screens, instead of opaque walls,
at both ends of the space help avoid visual
enclosure, maintaining the spatial ambiguity
characteristic of the *androne*.

After several renovations during its 300-year history, the palazzo of the Querini family had become isolated from its physical context, disengaged from the environmental conditions that had supported the logic of its design. Carlo Scarpa's renovation of the gardens and the first floor reactivates a reciprocity between building and landscape by conceptualizing the building as a receptacle that would contain the *acqua alta*—the highest tide—within its walls. This conception of architecture as a vessel for the engagement of landscape phenomena recognizes the role that cyclical fluctuations of water in Venice have had in shaping the city and its architecture.

In this project, natural phenomena and their representation are the locus for the construction of reciprocity between architecture and landscape. These relations of reciprocity operate at different scales, making the interior contingent on the exterior, the individual room on the urban fabric, and the local on the ecological. Scarpa's first set of operations recovers the spatial sequence of the traditional Venetian house, reversed during previous renovations, by rehabilitating the *androne*, the passageway that connects the canal at the front of the building to the courtyard at the rear, and reestablishing both pedestrian and gondola access from the S. Maria canal. Characteristic of the *androne* is its programmatic ambiguity: it is both an interior and an exterior space, partially exposed to the environment with the open courtyard at one end and the canal at the other, and subject to flooding. Recovering the canal-to-courtyard sequence allowed him to engage the canal within the interior of the building, to recuperate the spatial ambiguity of the *androne* and, ultimately, to conceive the interior of the building as a landscape.

(left) Water gates looking from causeway toward S. Maria canal. The gates reactivate canal access to the palazzo. From the gondola, the visitor climbs onto the causeway. This elevated pathway is parallel to the canal and is, during the *acqua alta*, surrounded by water on three sides.

(below left) Plan.

(bottom) Section.

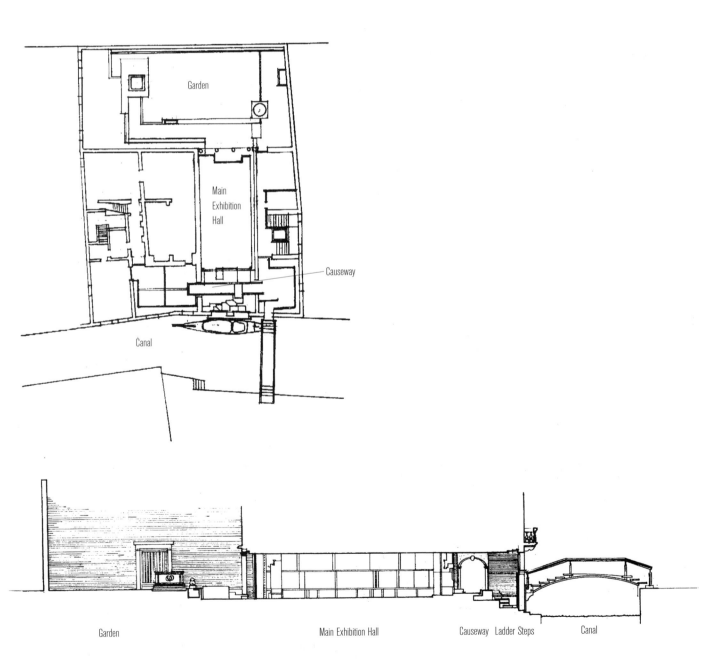

The ground floor of the Querini Stampalia Foundation is a landscape organized by a series of structures that direct the incoming water and control its movement within the building. Proposing one as the other—architecture as landscape—yields formal and representational shifts that challenge conventional roles assigned to each. The pathway that connects the entrance hall with the exhibition rooms is raised above the level of the water becoming, in effect, a causeway. A concrete curb surrounds the causeway and the entrance hall, and isolates the circulation and arrival spaces from the surrounding water. A moat separates the floor of the entrance hall from the original walls of the building. The northeast exhibition room functions also as a detention basin in case of extreme tidal fluctuation. Drainage channels inscribed in the floor of the northeast exhibition room and pipes that pierce through the exterior walls direct the water into the building and back to the canal when the tide recedes.

(top) Northeast exhibition hall; floor channels drain water back to the canal when tides recede.

(above) Moat around the entrance hall, separating the new, inserted, floor of the entrance hall from walls of the building.

(right) Ladder steps made of concrete with Istrian stone caps. The steps convey the visitor from the gondola to the causeway that connects the entrance hall with the exhibition spaces. The curb is continuous around the sides of the causeway, to gain access it is necessary to step over the curb.

Looking toward the palazzo from the garden.

If the building provides a reading of the landscape as natural phenomena with cycles that are beyond the control of humans, the garden offers the opposite interpretation. Protected from the tidal cycles, it exists as a cultivated haven, unburdened by unpredictable change. Here is a curious conceptual reversal of the traditional building-garden-landscape sequence established in the paradigm of the classical villa. Scarpa proposes the garden as the part of the project that is most removed from a "natural" condition. The building, engaged as it is with the tidal cycles, and conceptually dependent on them, is closer to nature.

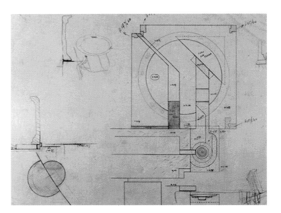

Studies for the design of the dry well.

Water is also the subject of the garden, but unlike the water inside the building, it is stable and idealized. It flows inside a canal across the width of the garden toward its conclusion into a dry well. The garden canal is elevated to the height of the sectional datum in the exhibition hall and in the causeway inside, signifying stability and, thus, difference from the fluctuating water of the city. Scarpa also gives the lawn the programmatic qualities usually associated with water, as a distanced surface where the visitor is not invited to walk, displacing circulation to the perimeter of the garden.

(left) Pool in garden. Channel for overflow is inscribed on the coping of the pool.

(below) Aerial view of garden.

Scarpa reinvents the building as an apparatus for measuring environmental change. The sectional datum inscribed in the interior, in the garden, in the ladder steps, and in the entrance bridge, is a measuring device akin to those elements in the city appropriated by the urban dweller as registers of change in the environment. As such, the palazzo's interior is both a fragment and microcosm of the city itself.

(top) Beginning of water channel in the garden. Its design references the labyrinthine network of canals that form the urban fabric of Venice.

(above) Pedestrian bridge. Its asymmetrical curvature registers a disparity between the grade at the sidewalk and at the building threshold.

(left) Ladder steps during *aqua alta*; the risers register water fluctuations.

LOYOLA LAW SCHOOL

Los Angeles, California, USA
1981–1984
Frank O. Gehry & Associates, Inc.

Frank Gehry has said about Loyola Law School that "this is not a site plan. I carefully unorganized it; I wanted it to look undesigned." This undesigned look does not constitute a denial of architecture. Rather, it reflects a layered and inclusive approach, with design sources ranging from the Acropolis to the Japanese dry garden at Ryoanji, and including paintings by Giorgio Morandi and Giorgio de Chirico.

Gehry initiated the project at a planning scale, countering his client's commission for a single building with a proposal to create a campus, to support the everyday life of the law school and to give it a more memorable identity. He then proceeded to dissolve and fragment this campus in order to make a landscape, producing an outdoor lobby of modulated interlocking spaces, each animated with multiple vistas. His solution resists a generalized collegiate identity of common lawn, as well as outdoor spaces that are merely leftover areas between buildings.

Looking from exterior stair of Burns Building
toward main stair and Merrifield Hall moot court.

Model, as seen from its Olympic Boulevard side, emphasizes building variety.

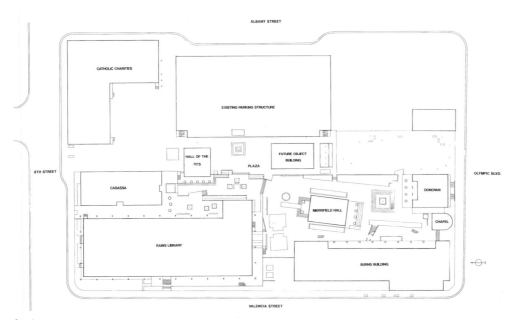

Site plan

Three strategies work together to establish a continuum of transformations between architecture and landscape in this restricted urban site. Two of these strategies invert the convention that associates architecture with figure and landscape with ground. A third strategy focuses attention on intermediate zones that are common to both architecture and landscape.

(right) Study model showing Burns Building (containing classrooms, offices, and student center) as ground.

(below) Sketch of Burns Building as ground for architecture and landscape objects.

One strategy is to treat landscape elements as architecture. Gehry first establishes a range of difference within the architecture that is broad enough to admit landscape, by varying the scale, style, and placement of the classroom, moot court, and chapel buildings that define and populate the space. He then introduces a series of landscape elements whose scale and variety parallel that of the small buildings, including a grass-covered pyramid and a pair of sloping grass planes, one of which is objectified by its unexpected freestanding condition. Gehry even makes a portion of the ground plane figural by collapsing onto it the same palette of grass outlined by white concrete that identifies the pyramid and the sloping planes. This gesture, which would seem merely graphic on its own, is part of a continuum from landscape-as-ground to landscape-as-object to building-as-object. Visible artifice is a precondition of landscape in this project; the continuum does not extend to naturalistic landscape elements.

In a second and complementary strategy, architecture relinquishes its claim to a figural identity in order to operate as landscape. The long flat elevation of the Burns Building seems both to mirror and to fold up the horizontal ground of the site. These two dimensionally similar surfaces—one vertical and the other horizontal—function together as a ground for the more objectlike architecture and landscape elements.

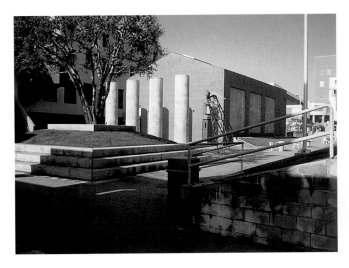

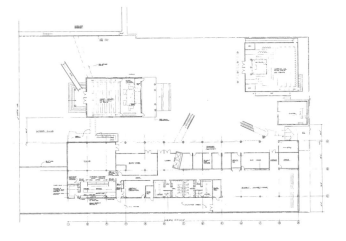

(top) View of freestanding grass sloped plane (right) and grass-covered pyramid, with Merrifield Hall beyond.

(above) First-floor plan of buildings, with landscape elements omitted.

(left) Looking toward Merrifield Hall from Olympic Boulevard entrance, with raked fire stair of Burns Building in foreground, showing variety of architectural and landscape objects and thresholds.

(above right) Sketch of thresholds

(right) Looking across the campus with freestanding colonnade-threshold of Donovan Hall at right.

The third strategy produces an intermediate class of artifacts that function as threshold zones between inside and outside, and between architecture and landscape. These include the freestanding porch, the courthouse steps, and the balcony of Donovan Hall overlooking Olympic Boulevard. The major contribution of the courthouse steps is often assumed to be their symbolic presence, but they also serve a critical social function, as they support and momentarily engage the space that flows through the site.

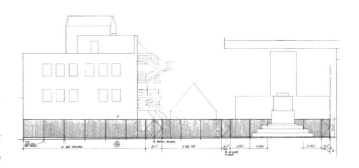

The stair that slices into the center of the Burns Building is a hybrid that plays multiple roles: it is a threshold element, a landscape figure, and an architecture ground, as well as (more conventionally) a landscape ground and architectural figure. It begins as a path inscribed in the horizontal plane of the site and culminates in the rooftop greenhouse pavilion. It links and activates both the horizontal and the vertical ground; it is part of the Burns Building, yet it is also one of the collection of objects that occupy the horizontal surface. It is an architectural promenade that includes diverse spatial events, particularly in the landings disengaged from the building.

It is possible to describe the reciprocity between architecture and landscape at Loyola in terms of a third thing—the urban. Gehry's project has been criticized as anti-urban for walling out the neighborhood with a security fence along Olympic Boulevard. Yet his design reveals more of the institution's identity, and contributes more to variety and scale of the street (that is otherwise lined with undistinguished commercial buildings) than would a single large building. In other words, he accommodates an institutional desire for security without producing a fortress. It is ironic that the preconception of outdoor space as "open" precludes an appreciation of the architecture's positive urban contributions.

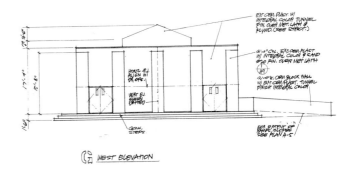

WEST ELEVATION

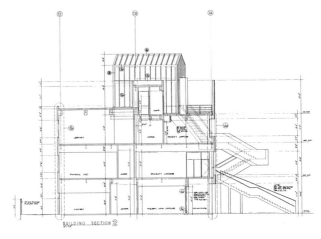

(top) Olympic Boulevard elevation showing overlap of Donovan Hall at security fence (balcony not shown).

(above middle) Olympic Boulevard elevation of Donovan Hall, showing balcony.

(above) Section through main stair at center of Burns Building.

(left) View from alongside Merrifield Hall, with Burns Building stair at right.

VILLA DALL' AVA

St. Cloud, France
1984–1991
Rem Koolhaas, Office for Metropolitan Architecture

The Villa Dall'Ava appears, especially in photographs, to be a single building. In fact, it is a constellation of elements: a glass house partially recessed into the earth, a rooftop swimming pool, and two metal-clad apartments. The architecture's apparent singularity is both its solution and its problem—solution because it holds everything together, problem because it conceals the complexity of its spatial identity. It functions as an alibi, facilitating the project's acceptance within conventional frameworks of architectural interpretation, while Koolhaas pursues his interest in landscape, or what he calls the "unbuilt."

For Koolhaas, "landscape became an important issue (with the Villa Dall'Ava) because . . . the specifics became more accessible. You can read the house in its entirety with the landscape." (Davis, 1996) The small footprint of the house, down the middle of its long narrow lot, reflects his effort to relate it to its suburban neighborhood, and to allow its context to have the greatest impact. This impact is reflected in the architect's perception that photographs that best represent the project are taken from the interior looking out.

(right) First floor plan

(below right) Ground floor plan

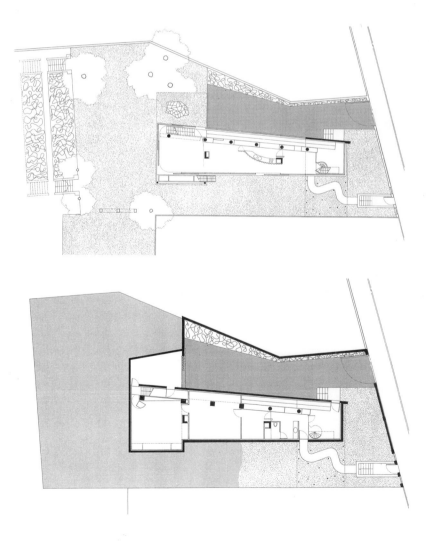

Looking into the house from the north, at the
layered horizontal and vertical surfaces
that engage the space across the weather wall.
The plywood wall of the ramp articulates a
volume of inside-outside space in concert with a
tree, a column, and the metal-clad underside of
the apartment.

View of south side of house along lawn.

The project negotiates its sloping topography with four different sectional configurations. Two of these sections are interior routes that begin in the foyer: the spiral stair that climbs to the dining area, and the ramp to the living room. Two are exterior: the sloping lawn along the south that leads from the portico to the backyard, and the one-story-high concrete retaining wall that delineates the edge between the yard and the driveway. The similar topographical articulation of the ramp and the yard, on the one hand, and the driveway and the foyer, on the other, renders less singular the opposition of inside and outside.

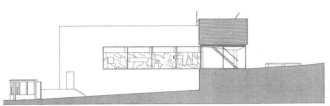

(top) Section through entry and yard at south side of house, showing elevation.

(above) Section through yard at north side of house showing relation between apartment and retaining wall at driveway.

(left) Detail at intersection of retaining wall and living room at north side of house.

(bottom left) Longitudinal section through the ramp, yard, apartments, and pool.

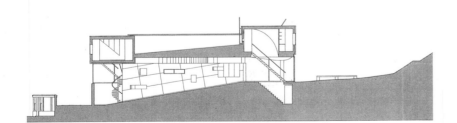

The villa has two primary instances of architecture-becoming-landscape. One is the floating pool, which asserts the roof as a second ground plane. This displacement calls into question both the identity of the pool as landscape and the house as architecture, initiating a paradoxical space that is simultaneously involved with house, garden, neighborhood, and city. As well as being a structural feat, and a dramatic culmination of the several routes through the house, this roof landscape makes visible scales of site that are imperceptible at ground level. One of these is a neighborhood scale, that crosses property lines, in which nearby pools and tennis courts constitute a series to which the floating pool belongs. The other, a metropolitan scale, constructs the roof landscape as a foreground for the Eiffel Tower–embellished Parisian skyline to the east.

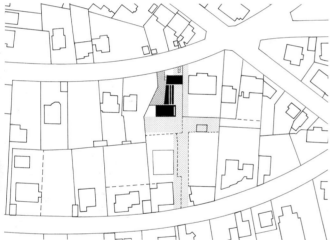

(above) Looking east from the roof, across pool.

(top left) Looking west from the roof toward a neighboring pool and house.

(above left) Location plan

(far left) Sketch, by Yves Brunier, of the garden as seen from the living room.

(left) Space defined by the overhanging apartment, the ground plane edge at the retaining wall, living room curtain, and ramp wall.

The second major architecture-becoming-landscape event is the radical engagement of interior and exterior space where the living room meets the garden. Glass doors and curtains retract to open the northwest corner as well as the entire back of the house. This breaking open the envelope of enclosure is enhanced by the canopylike presence of the metal-clad apartment overhead. A metal stair physically connects these two spatial events—the roof landscape and the garden living room—through the transparencies of the house.

View across the living room toward the garden, showing how the open corner joins interior and exterior space.

The strategy of spatial displacement also disrupts the identity of numerous individual elements, calling into question whether they belong to architecture or landscape. This breakdown of preconceived identities facilitates the construction (by architect and inhabitant) of new ones. One way Koolhaas constructs identity is to develop surfaces, both horizontal and vertical, that take spatial advantage of—and represent—their layering and their two-sidedness. These surfaces hold the project together in the face of its multiple displacements. Even transparent planes register, represent, and form spaces on two sides, some of which would ordinarily be residual in this suburban context. This multidirectional conception explores how an architectural surface differs from the skin of a body, that is visible only from the outside.

Koolhaas's reciprocal operations reframe the suburban condition in urban terms, and still respect its particular spatiality. For this architect, to be urban is "to create a larger entity with things that are usually not seen in relationship to each other."(Davis, 1996) In this spirit, the project fragments in order to reconnect, but in reconnecting shifts emphasis to previously unconsidered relationships.

Shadow of a tree on the south façade of the house.

(above left) Looking west to backyard, from the pole forest at the entry to the lower level.

(above right) Looking out from the dining area: the grove of poles that marks the villa's threshold possesses a different but equally strong spatial presence from the dining room interior, appearing to be a "pulling apart" of the bamboo-and-glass layered wall in the foreground.

SCHOOL AT MORELLA

Morella, Spain
1986–1993
Carmen Pinós and Enric Miralles, Achitects

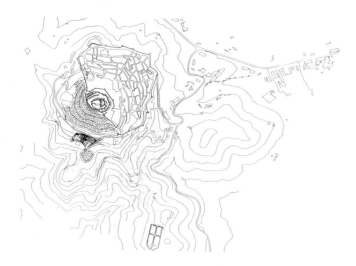

(above) Site plan. The school is sited at the base of the fortified town of Castellón, overlooking a landscape of terraced hills.

(below) View from ramp between classroom and dormitory buildings to distant hills.

At the School at Morella, Carmen Pinós and Enric Miralles construct a precise choreography of architecture, building site, and landscape. This precision begins with the architects' hypersensitive siting of the building, which then supports other strategies that unveil ambiguities between inside and outside. These startegies are the inversion of the figure ground relationship, the use of movement as a device to initiate spatial and visual relations between architecture and landscape, and shifts in the relationship of the subject to the view.

The siting of the school complex repeats the historical development of the hill town, as it expanded over time toward the best orientation: classrooms descend the hill on the outer, exposed, side, rotated to face the sun, and dormitories descend along the inner, protected, side. The distribution of program within the school precinct is also analogous to the "in-between" condition of the site: classrooms and dormitories demarcate the location of the school toward the hill town, while common spaces, both indoor and outdoor, form the exterior—landscape—limit of the site at different levels. Both building and outdoor spaces follow closely the topography of the terrain. These site-planning strategies dissolve the perimeter of the school precinct so that it becomes interwoven with its context. However, they are not motivated by an interest in contextualism, as evidenced by the use of modern, prefabricated construction materials, but are the necessary precondition for establishing a reciprocity that breaks down distinctions between inside and outside.

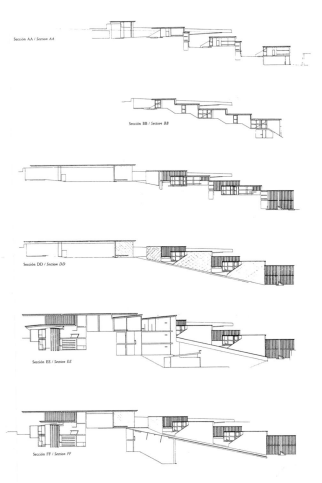

Sección AA / Section AA

Sección BB / Section BB

Sección DD / Section DD

Sección EE / Section EE

Sección FF / Section FF

(above) View from classroom building terrace towards Castellón, showing the similarities in form, scale, and color of the façades of the dormitory building and the topographical characteristics of the hill town.

(left) Longitudinal sections

(below) The exterior is also brought into the interior through the terrace furniture and pavement in the interior common areas.

The accommodation of architectual program into steep terrain creates leftover spaces that are typically left to absorb unreconciled building geometries. At the School at Morella, these spaces, instead of being a by-product of the figure, generate the overall form of the building. Terraces, ramps, and private dormitory gardens are emphasized to become figure. These grounds, usually the passive repositories of buildings, are reconceived as figured voids that actively function to fragment the volumes of the building, to create fissures, gaps, views, and passage between and through, in order to provoke its relationship with the landscape.

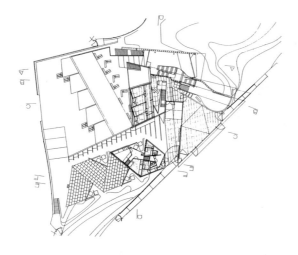
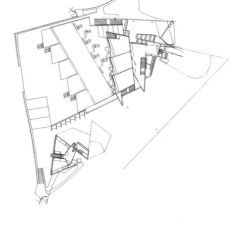
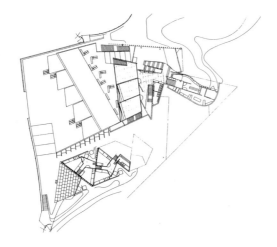
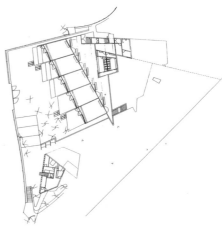

(clockwise from top left)

Upper access plan

Level two plan

Level three plan (garden)

Level one plan

Carmen Pinós has said that the first impulse was "to mark off our precinct with a path, that is at the same time a building..."(Curtis, 1991) The project is conceived as a series of trajectories that describe and delimit, but without limiting, a territory in which inside and outside are invisibly woven. In this architectural promenade, interior and exterior are continuous in time. This spatial continuum transforms architecture from a graspable object into a medium that both crystallizes and invents site. The figural and spatial prominence given to horizontal and vertical circulation, both inside and outside, further breaks down the building's autonomy, by substituting for a purely architectural presence one made of passing encounters between architecture and landscape.

ÆCCION A

ÆCCION B

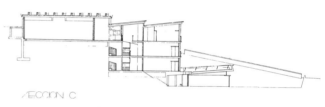

ÆCCION C

(above) Sections

(left) View of the interior of the classroom building showing voids, vertical fenestration, and light permeating the space from all directions.

(below) Ambiguity is evident upon arrival: from this point, the predominant element is the roof, not the façade, leading the eye to the distant horizon.

(above) The insistent use of stairs and ramps, and the accompanying shifts of viewpoint and topographical positioning, engage the visitor in two ways: physically, through movement, and visually, through exposure to views.

(below) Topographical study of school precinct

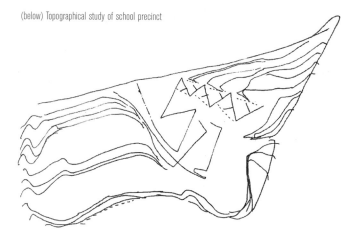

Ambiguity is further augmented by the inverson of commonly held expectations about exterior and interior space. Outside, visitors are made to feel protected from the landscape, as if inside. This is accomplished by positioning the visitor always in relation to a building wall or a roof overhang. Benches are never positioned in the conventional way, at the outer edge, parapet, or rail of an open terrace. This position of being at the edge of a view is, paradoxically, always reserved for the inside of the building, where the visitor is meant to feel as if outside, suspended in the landscape. Inside, the visual experience is also akin to that outside: there are no opaque walls to interrupt vision; it is allowed to escape in all directions. Likewise, light comes in from all sides, as if outdoors, and is supplemented by additional artificial lighting when needed to further emphasize a sense of exterior inside.

The views from the architectural promenade are filtered, layered, fragmented and multiple: in the interior they are always given in small amounts, through the vertically articulated fenestration; on the exterior, emphasis is on views through the gaps between buildings. The traditional gaze over a silent, composed, and passive landscape is here transformed to allow a reciprocal exchange in which the landscape may not be always benign, nor the viewer always dominant.

(left) View through gap between classroom building and dormitory building.

(below) View uphill from classroom building terrace.

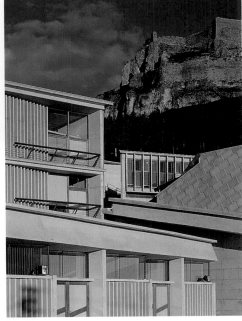

BARNES RESIDENCE

Nanaimo, British Columbia, Canada
1990–1992
Patkau Architects

A strategy of looking for difference leads, in the work of Patkau Architects, to a search for instances of the local and the particular. In the Barnes Residence these instances become embedded in its architecture through the application of two landscape architectural strategies. The first is a picturesque strategy that conceptualizes the project as a trajectory through landscape and architectural space that unfolds, reveals, and re-presents aspects of the site. The second is a site-specific strategy that embeds this trajectory into the particularities of the place, by bringing closer and making real landscapes that are also, paradoxically, made distant through the construction of views. The two strategies are interwoven and shift among different scales, resulting in an architecture that is in measured relation to the immediate and the corporeal, as well as to the distant and the abstract.

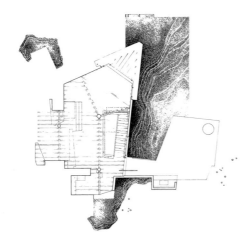

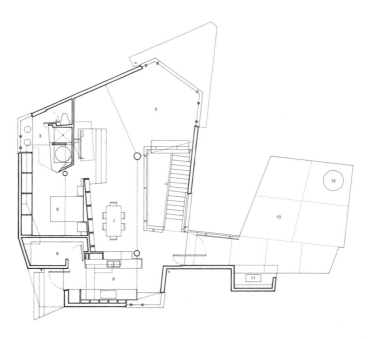

(above) Main-floor plan

(above left) Plan drawing showing relationship of building to rock outcrops.

(right) Exterior view from the northwest. The particularities of the rocks' scale and shape are measured by the walls that deform at the bottom to meet the irregular topography of the site. This deformation contrasts with the clean unbroken lines of the top of the wall.

The house occupies a provocative point on the site: a tight space between two rock outcroppings. This siting of the building, along with the siting of the parking terrace at a much lower elevation, establishes a topographical theme in the architectural promenade that begins at grade in the parking terrace, and ends at canopy level in the living room. In the exterior of the building, the topographical theme is revealed in the stucco-clad walls that adjust their position and angles to fit between, over, and above the rock outcrops. Once inside the front door, measured changes in the visitor's position vis-à-vis the outcrop internalize the site's topography, reconstructing it through architectural means within the space of the building. The insertion of site-specific events that reveal the transformation of the building as it engages the site transforms the modernist notion of the architectural promenade, which engages the landscape primarily through the device of the distant view. Through shifts in and juxtapositions of scale, the project weaves local events with abstract architectural space, constructing spatial differentiations between the tactile and conceptual aspects of the landscape.

(top) Two low square windows focus the view from the foyer out towards the moss-covered rocks. Only the thickness of the glass separates the visitor's legs from the moist soft texture of the moss.

(right) View from the top of the stairs, to the left, out onto the terrace. The terrace sits directly on top of the rock outcrop. The forest, the rocky terrain underfoot, and views of the Strait of Georgia—the geographic center of the region—are simultaneously experienced from the terrace.

Site specificity is the basis of another architectural strategy of Patkau Architects: the insertion of totemic elements, which the architects have defined as "highly developed components within a generic space that create identifiable and differentiated places within the building."(Carter, 1994). In this house, the totemic elements include polished concrete columns with metal diagonal braces that support the roof, and the roof itself, which is designed as a continuous surface that hovers over the interior space of the house. Together, these elements reference the forest and its canopy, and the history of timber production in this landscape, as region-specific elements within the interior of the building.

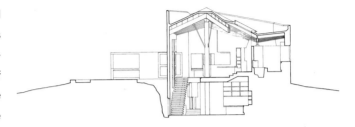

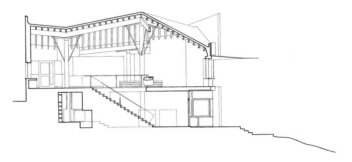

(top) Composite transverse section.

(above) Composite longitudinal section.

(left) "Worm's-eye" axonometric of living room ceiling.

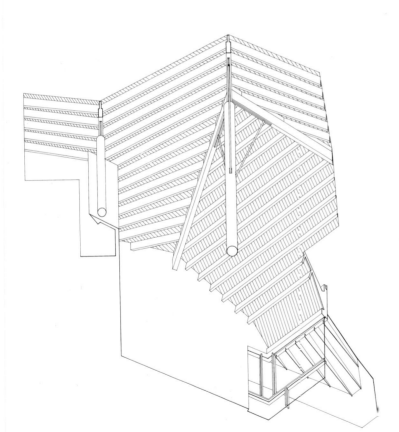

Patkau Architects' pursuit of the particular leads to heterogeneity of space and form. In the Barnes Residence heterogeneity is found in the simultaneous presence of orthogonal and non-orthogonal geometry, in the different figural strengths of each façade, and in the change of materials to reflect a change in the structural function of the part. It is also evident in the way the totemic elements render the building spatially uneven, by emphasizing the events that constitute difference.

(above) East façade. Heterogeneity is revealed in the different visual strengths of the façades, each a response to the particularities of program and orientation.

(right) Exterior from the northwest at night.

Heterogeneity also relates the Barnes Residence to the landscape in conceptual ways. In ecological terms, heterogeneity, or diversity, refers to a structural complexity in which each part contributes in specific and different ways to its larger system. The Barnes Residence suggests that reciprocity between architecture and landscape can be based on the application of principles of relatedness, rather than on stylistic translations from one to the other. Acknowledging that each of its component parts contributes in different ways to the whole liberates the work from the conceptual limitations of formal strategies that would merely blend building and landscape, and creates an architecture that exists in mutuality with the natural world.

MATERIALITY

The operation of materiality displaces matter from its traditional position as "base" at the service of form, to become significant content of the work. It is concerned with the ways that materials induce form to be thought, and how matter can be a generator of sense. It has less to do with the beauty of materials than with how they operate—to index and express temporality, to represent site, or to support a phenomenological reading of a place.

In the projects presented here, materiality "disprivileges" form but does not necessarily deny it. Some projects, such as the Igualada Cemetery and the Stone House are formally powerful, but in all of these projects form is, at least in part, at the service of matter. A project such as the Thomson Factory—where plant succession is allowed to take its course—becomes, through time, formless.

Because architecture and landscape architecture explicitly share the operation of reconfiguring matter, it is worthwhile to explore how this commonality affects their inter-relation. At Herzog & De Meuron's Stone House in Tavole, Italy, both the building and the existing garden contribute to the same reading of the site's terraced structure and dry-laid stone wall constructions. Architecture's dialogue with the local stone—within a reinforced concrete frame—offers a phenomenological interpretation of the materiality of the site, and of its translation into construction.

The operation of materiality is about the disclosure of different kinds of knowledge of natural and cultural worlds through the arrangement of materials in form and space. The Bamboo Garden, for instance, explicitly displays technical and historical knowledge—of hydrology, botany, agriculture, climate, and so on. This display represents a kind of abstraction that is not formal, but instead operates through the displacement of elements from their native contexts. By planting species of bamboo that are marginally hardy in the region of Paris, Chemetoff not only represents the microclimatic advantage that has been gained by sinking the garden, but also discloses his own knowledge of centuries-old practices of French garden-making.

The landscape architects for the Thomson Factory bring forth temporal aspects of materiality to create and represent a procedure through which to construct an ecosystem. The project exists as physical traces of successional stages, countering the typical hierarchy

that privileges the permanent over the temporary. Because no one event is considered the ideal state of the project, there are no preconceptions about what the landscape should look like. Instead, it is positively cast as ever-changing. In this case, the operation of materiality induces what Michel Foucault calls a condition of "exteriority," (Foucault, 1971) by which he means that the subject focuses on the physical reality of the work, rather than trying to discern some hidden meaning within it. This conceptual shift allows nature to play an active role, rather than to be the passive means of a program of representation.

Materiality acquires a different sense when the program is a cemetery, with its material content of corpses. In the two cemeteries presented here, the indexing and expression of conditions of being, that is, of life, growth, aging, and death, imply parallels between corporeal and vegetative material states. The architects of these projects work with materials as assemblages that have the capacity to act in precise ways: to establish continuity with the site, or react to weather or to another material, or to link designer and participant. The projects exist in the accumulation of material renderings of ideas and actions, rather than in any individual instance. This accumulation sometimes brings into focus unexpected qualities of a material, as in the Brion Cemetery, where the transparency of water, a material property, becomes visible because elements beneath its surface draw the eye downward. An individual uses the knowledge gained through the material aspects of the project to perform the conceptual joining of its pieces, to arrive at a multifaceted understanding of the work.

The different ways in which the operation of materiality functions imply different modes of subject-object relations. In one, exemplified by the Brion Cemetery, materiality is aligned with an iconographic program. In another one, exemplified by the Thomson Factory, materiality is not aligned with any additional program of signification. In each case, the epistemological basis of the operation requires shifting from a purely visual kind of knowledge to one that includes physicality, engaging a subject through the constructional logic of the work rather than through the contemplation of its forms.

BRION CEMETERY

San Vito d'Altivole, Treviso, Italy
1967-1978
Carlo Scarpa, Architect

Commissioned by the industrialist Brion, this L-shaped walled funerary garden precinct wraps the northeast corner of a small cemetery at the edge of a village in the Veneto. Scarpa presents the cemetery as a space through which to explore relationships between the eternal and the transitory. He achieves his specific version of materiality through two related strategies that operate at different scales. One is the use of montage to integrate heterogeneous elements. The other is an emphasis on the joints between these elements as a kind of "tectonic condensation" (Frampton, 1995). Together, these strategies produce a fragmentary composition, in which focus is consistently displaced from form to matter, and from formation to transformation.

Scarpa's version of transformation accords an equivalent presence to different states, thereby allowing matter and space to condition each other: neither is dominant, neither establishes the "facts" of the project that the other must adhere to. This transformative equivalence of matter and space provides an allegory of the cemetery's programmatic content—the dematerializing bodies within the tombs.

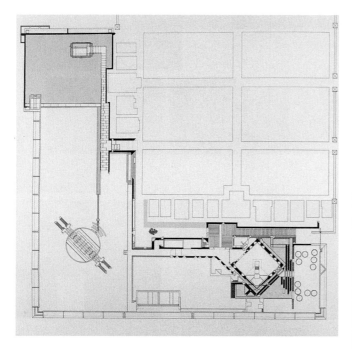

(above) Plan

(left) Viewed from outside, the inward-sloping concrete boundary wall of the Brion precinct, with its open corner that allows views out; the chapel and cypress grove are visible above the wall.

(left) A water trough borders the chapel along the concrete-and-grass entry walkway.

(below) Section through Brion precinct and Municipal Cemetery, facing *Propylaeum*.

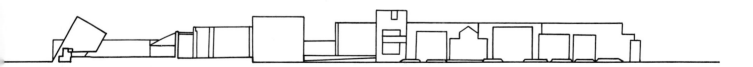

This shifting equivalence of matter and space means that nothing in the cemetery is completely separable as an object. Apparently solid matter always "leads" somewhere, folding over to reveal another not completely visible or knowable space. Elements that seem to be freestanding objects, such as the tombs, each connect to either a horizontal or vertical ground. The chapel itself is merely a fragment of interior space, a hinge that gathers its light from cracks that communicate with adjacent outdoor spaces. The only freestanding building is the "hooded" meditation pavilion, but this is also a freestanding ground, bounded by water. Its radical separateness provides a distance across which to reflect on the tomb of the Brion couple, which is visible only through a slit in the hood.

Like his drawings, Scarpa's projects achieve their complexity through the stratification of successive overlays, within which interrelationships and intersections between scales are discovered. Pierluigi Nicolin has described his way of working as a kind of "parallel action"—an indirect approach to building that produces a "part for whole" mode of figuration. This parallel action operates not only within the project but also at the scale of the site, in the way that, according to the architect, the cemetery garden "capture[s] the sense of the countryside" (Nicolin, 1983).

(top) *Propylaeum* interior, showing the upward shift of horizon to focus on intersecting circles with layers of ground beyond.

(above) At first sight, the *Propylaeum* appears similar to the dark openings of the family mausoleums that ring the cemetery, suggesting that it too is a caesura that will incorporate the visitor into an unknown interior.

(right) Looking through the truncated circular opening into the chapel interior, with the altar, at right, and the door to the priests' garden, at left.

(below right) Section through Municipal Cemetery and Brion precinct at *Propylaeum*, looking north toward *Arcosolium*. Note the raised ground and inward-sloping boundary wall of Brion precinct.

(left) Ground is displaced from a horizontal to a
vertical position in the thickened concrete wall
next to Scarpa's tomb. It accommodates layers of
earth and small trees.

(below) View of Scarpa's tomb, joined to the Brion
precinct with the thickened wall, layered with
earth and trees.

(bottom) Detail of the raised concrete "tray" of
lawn, with the boundary wall at left.

Scarpa calls attention to materials by displacing them from their conventional posi-
tions. This technique of displacement is one aspect of an anti-essentializing
approach, which compels the visitor to look again at familiar things. Within the Brion
precinct, ground becomes figure, disrupting the conventional hierarchy of
figure/ground. Scarpa raises and objectifies the ground as monolithic trays, separated from the inward-leaning boundary walls by a gap. Brick paths cut through the
raised earth, making space for the visitor's body, paralleling the way that the tombs
carve out space for their occupants.

Both tombs, one for the Brion couple and the other for their relations, are recessed within the ground and, at the same time, still on its surface; each creates a field of space around itself. Scarpa has hybridized two burial methods: digging into the earth to position sarcophagi that are usually placed above ground. This play between depth, mass, space, and surface challenges the acceptance of a surface as "truth," and calls into question what constitutes a surface. The tomb of the Brion husband and wife—what he called the *Arcosolium*—opens the ground to reconstruct it as layers of earth, concrete, and plants. A large lowered arch protects a shallow depression in the earth without creating closure. Beneath it, two sarcophagi lean toward each other, floating on rounded bases, their relationship to the ground destabilized.

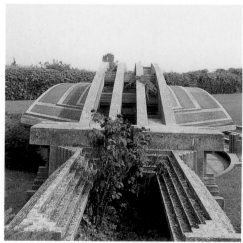

(clockwise from top left)
Arcosolium seen from the family tomb.

Brion sarcophagi on rounded bases within
Arcosolium.

View of *Arcosolium* as layers of reconstructed
ground, made up of earth, concrete, and plants.

Study of *Arcosolium*.

Scarpa questions the fixed identity of materials as well as surfaces, by combining them in ways that reveal their unexpected properties. Concrete only partially disappears beneath the surface of the still water in the pool around the chapel, its stratifications visible in the depths as if in another, long-forgotten world. Thus, water as a material is demonstrated to possess a visual permeability reminiscent of the architect's drawings. Plant materials also play a spatial role, layering and interweaving with each other in ways that emphasize their individual properties: the rounded form of the yews, and the weeping one of the spruce, the strong perfumes of the lilacs and roses, and the somber darkness of the cypresses. Vines assailing the tombs index an inevitable destruction of both form and matter. A forsythia, the first plant to bloom in the spring, is planted by Scarpa's tomb.

(top) A brick-surfaced path cuts between concrete-contained masses of earth, with the stair to the *Arcosolium* at left; to reach the *Arcosolium*, one must leave the path, climb a few stairs, and walk across the grass.

(above middle) Detail of the stepping stones leading from the chapel to the cypress grove, showing the transparent depths of the pool.

(above) Detail of the intersection of building and ground at the chapel colonnade.

(left) In contrast to the still water surrounding the chapel, a slow-moving stream flows in a channel from the reflecting pool to just above the *Arcosolium*, as if to irrigate the tomb.

STONE HOUSE

Tavole, Italy
1985–1988
Herzog and De Meuron

In Herzog and De Meuron's Stone House the continuity between architecture—as artifice—and landscape—as nature—is based on their shared materiality. Both the building and the garden terraces are formed by gathering stones from the surrounding landscape and reconfiguring them in multiple ways, presenting garden and architecture as part of the same set of interventions in the physical world. This continuity between architecture and landscape does not originate in an interest in mimesis or regionalism. The architects' careful observation of the surrounding landscape is not to assimilate its visual qualities, but to understand, and ultimately reveal through construction, phenomenological aspects of its materiality.

Transactions between landscape and architecture begin on the façades of the building, where the architects locate most apparently their phenomenological reading of the site's dry-laid stone walls. On the façades, the surfaces of the stone and exposed-concrete structure are coplanar, making the surface of the façade flat. The relationship between the stones and the structure is most significantly expressed in the way the corner concrete column is concealed behind the façade, allowing the stone surfaces to continue uninterrupted around the corner of the building. This diminishes the reading of the concrete's structural function and diverts attention to the stone, now reassembled on the building like the dry-laid walls of the landscape.

What at first may seem like a mimetic gesture that transfers a landscape image onto a façade is belied by subtle indications of the stone's nonbearing function. The stones are not battered, as they are in the landscape, where they have to support the retained soil's weight. Additionally, the concrete structure that remains exposed horizontally and vertically at the center of all façades points to its structural function. The suppression of both the purely functional and the purely compositional redefines the identity of architectural elements and their materials. Thus, the stones, although in reality a cladding, take on the spirit of a load-bearing wall. The concrete beams at each floor replicate a feeling of ground, onto which a stone wall is built. The concealment of the concrete structure at the corner negates its potential role as boundary and further eliminates hierarchy from the surface by blurring the distinction between frame and infill.

(above) West façade at the terrace. The stone and the concrete frame are assembled to emphasize the construction of a surface, rather than the expression of mass.

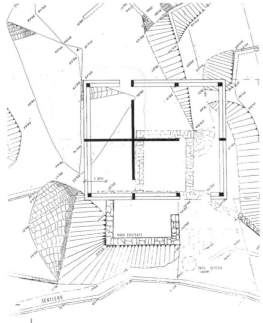

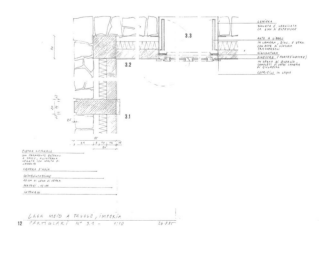

(above) Partial exterior view from the south. The coherence of the façade has less to do with constructional necessities, and more to do with a phenomenological reading of its materials.

(right) Site plan

(far right) Construction detail showing corner support hidden behind face of building.

(above) Transition from house to terrace.

(left) South elevation

(below right) East façade. The figurative equality between the stones and the concrete structure presents them in an ambiguous relationship with each other: one is never the background for the other.

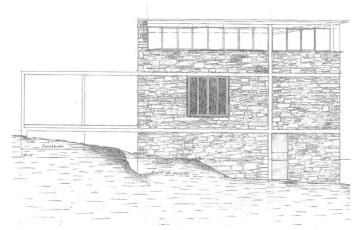

The strategy of assigning the same value to things that typically exist in a formal or functional hierarchy is present in other aspects of the building. Centrality and symmetry have been suppressed in the façade, where windows and doors are incorporated into the texture of the surface. The architects question the traditional relationship between horizontal and vertical planes by creating a formal correspondence between plan and elevation. This is achieved through the inscription of the figure of a cross in the façades of the building, as well as in the plans of the ground level and first floor. In the exterior walls, the cross is the exposed reinforced-concrete structure. In the floor plans, it is the walls that separate the four rooms of the space. Their exact correspondence asserts the equivalency of the ground to the figure in the building.

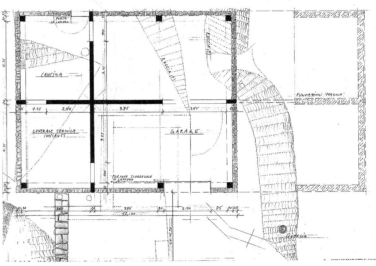

(above) Ground-floor plan

(left) Conceptual sketch of the building wall.

Continuity between architecture and landscape also takes on more overtly physical gestures, such as a topographical equivalency between interior floor and exterior ground. By locating the building so that it engages one of the existing terraces on the site, the ground level and first floor assume the terrace elevations, becoming continuous with the existing site topography. The continuity of the ground plane between inside and outside is then restated by the pergola, which is the extension of the reinforced-concrete structure of the house beyond the façade. Resting directly on the terrace, it joins ground with figure and site with construction.

Exterior view from the southeast

(above right) Transverse section, showing existing wall.

(right) Longitudinal section, showing continuation of ground plane at first floor.

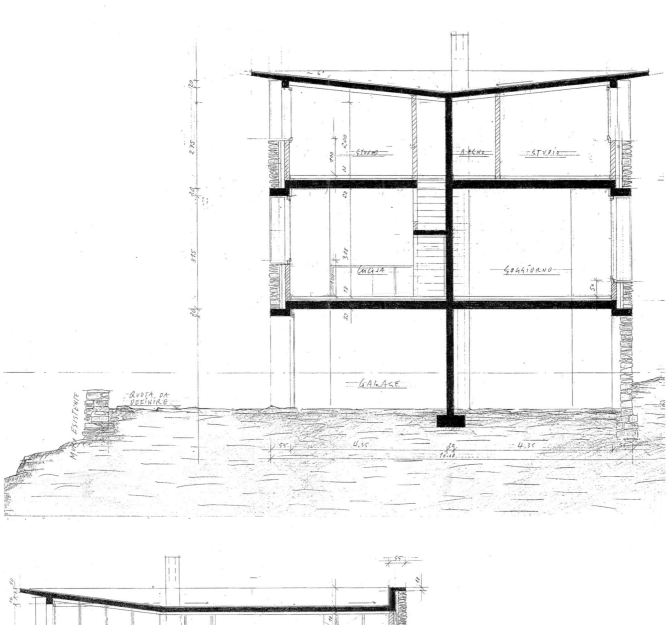

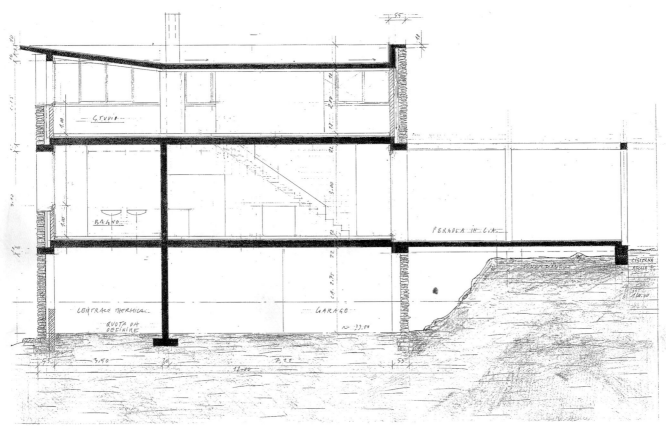

BAMBOO GARDEN

Parc de la Villette, Paris, France
1986–1989
Alexandre Chemetoff, Bureau des Paysages

The Bamboo Garden, the fourth in the sequence of thematic gardens along the *cinematic promenade* of the Parc de la Villette in Paris, introduces the aleatory and the unforeseeable into the systemic landscape of Bernard Tschumi's park. Lowered to a depth of five meters below the flat surface of the park, the garden reveals what the park chooses to ignore: climate, earth, cycles of water, and the networks of complexity that characterize the urban landscape. The Bamboo Garden produces and exhibits knowledge about the natural world. In other words, it activates an operation of materiality.

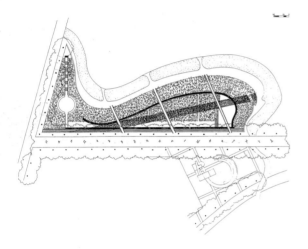

(above) Plan

(right) View from the garden toward the park above.

(above) View of the garden from the park above.
To the left is one of Bernard Tschumi's follies,
next to the sycamore allée that forms part of his
cinematic promenade.

(below) View of the bridge in the *cinematic
promenade* of the Parc de la Villette from inside
the bamboo garden.

(right) Detail of the water channel. To the right is the beginning of Daniel Buren's band of pavement and bamboo.

(below) Collected in gutters suspended from the retaining wall, the water empties into a canal that circulates around the perimeter of the garden. The water is then recycled to irrigate the garden and to humidify its environment: jets placed on high points are turned on at regularly scheduled intervals.

Chemetoff's primary operative technique is the disclosure of structural relationships between the elements of the garden. All elements are contingent upon the others, and these multiple contingencies are categorically demonstrated. The decision to lower the level of the garden below that of the park has hydrological and climatic consequences that are not only revealed, but become the subject of the garden. The first consequence is the immediate need for a retaining wall. Its numerous weep holes, generously dimensioned, reveal the presence of a high water table, due to leaks from the nearby canal. This surplus of water coming through the wall requires, in turn, the organization of a water cycle in the garden that conveys water from the wall to its eventual end in the garden's irrigation system.

The retaining wall faces south and reflects heat from the sun into the space of the garden, creating a local microclimate that is warmer than the one outside the garden. The bamboo, indigenous to warmer environments, openly display this fact. The lowered garden is also relatively sheltered from the noise of the surrounding environment, a condition demonstrated in Bernhard Leitner's antechamber to the garden. The bamboo, the retaining wall, and the heightened sounds are representations of the localized conditions of the environment, but they are representations that convey meaning through materials, rather than through form.

(above) Detail of the bamboo forest floor.

(below left) Bernhard Leitner's antechamber to the garden. The cylindrical space augments the subtle sounds of the garden, like those of dripping, moving water.

(below) Interior of the garden, showing the water channel.

The lowered garden also reveals the network of infrastructure that crisscrosses the city underground. The pipes that travel suspended over the garden point to the ground as mass rather than as mere surface. Daniel Buren's band of pavement and bamboo that cuts through the garden is both a reference to these infrastructure networks within the earth, and an elaboration of the themes begun by Chemetoff—the chain of events that are unleashed in a space as the result of introducing a new element.

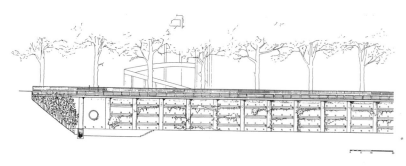

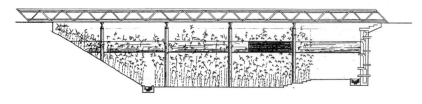

(clockwise from above left) In the garden, view of layers of infrastructure

Partial section

Cross section

The irregularity of treads is accentuated by the uneven length of the step risers, which also describe the uneven curvature of the slope.

In opposition to the park, which generalizes by applying an abstract framework equally throughout the site, the garden is about comprehending and measuring small differences in the environment (Auricoste, 1987). The steps on the curved entrance path have treads of different lengths, describing the irregular profile of the embankment. Also recording the particular, the forty varieties of bamboo display a wide spectrum of green tones, configurations of trunk rings, and textures. Similarly, the different tones on the pebbles of Daniel Buren's band point to their different geographical origins. Black basalt from the Ardèche contrasts with gray gravel from the Rhône. The Bamboo Garden is an accumulation of material renderings that together provide knowledge of the place.

The dialectic between the park and the garden is reiterated in the opposition created between the sunny, predominantly mineral, south-facing wall, and the shady, predominantly vegetal, north-facing slope. The wall engages the park above as it describes aspects of its subsurface condition. The forest of bamboo affirms the garden's material autonomy from the park. The three bridges suspended over the garden allow the continuity of the cinematic promenade in the park above, and the spatial autonomy of the garden below. Finally, whereas from the promenade the garden is a scene—a distant, framed view in the cinematic sequence—Chemetoff's material renderings of the garden stand against the contemplative implications of the promenade, and reveal the biological complexity of the site. The meaning of the garden lies in the knowledge it produces through its material and constructional logic, and not in the contemplative aspects of its forms.

(above) Detail of the walk with dwarf variety of bamboo.

(below left) View along the length of the retaining wall showing the predominantly mineral south-facing edge of the garden, and the predominantly vegetal north-facing slope.

IGUALADA CEMETERY

Igualada, Spain
1985–1991
Enric Miralles & Carmen Pinós, Architects

The Igualada Cemetery is a place of stillness that has been created, paradoxically, through an architecture in continual movement. Its massive, clifflike concrete burial chamber walls define a space that winds through a rough landscape of ravines, rocks, and pines. The provocative forms of the project are grounded in their materiality, but this concreteness does not produce certainty. Instead, the architects' agile manipulation of matter destabilizes conventional meanings into a web of signification that resonates between site and body, living and dead.

The material treatment of the ground at Igualada opens up thresholds of meaning in many directions. In this project, "ground" is a concept that unifies past and present, site and program, in a myriad of real and invented traces that the architects have developed into a network of overlapping exchanges. Because of its precious content of bodies, the ground merits figuration, as in the termination of the burial-chamber wall at the circular plaza. The visitor's body seems to participate in forming the ground, entering to descend into the main space of the cemetery through the two flights of concrete stairs tunneled into the earth from the level of the chapel. This suggestion of a moving body's active role in the formation of the project echoes one of Miralles' myth-narratives of its origins, as if a "giant's finger had drawn a line through the earth." (Miralles, 1994.)

Looking southeast at the entry level, with the stair canopy in the foreground.

(above) View from the north end of the
cemetery; the incision is built on three levels, two
of which are cut into the ground. The stepped
two-story burial chamber walls rise from the main
plaza at the lowest level of the cemetery.

(below) Model

(below right) Site plan of the entire cemetery, of
which a portion has been built.

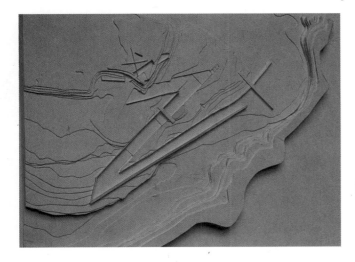

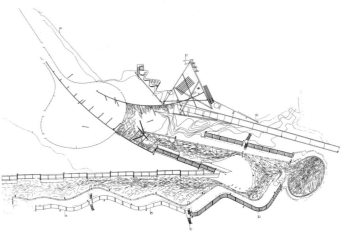

(below) Construction view of incision looking north.

(bottom) Meeting of burial chamber walls with
sloping ground plane.

The project's sectional logic articulates material presences in terms of their construction, rather than as beautiful surfaces that cover hidden depths. The cut also represents a probe into the site and its memories, through which the architects explore the site's qualities while reorganizing them, making sense out of the intensely geological character of this stratified terrain, previously a quarry. They have made visible and palpable the relationship between the site's past and present programs: that a quarry and a cemetery both involve cutting into the ground, although one is a place of removal from the earth in order to build elsewhere, while the other is a place of return to it.

(above) Existing site conditions showing layers of exposed geological strata.

(left) Site sections

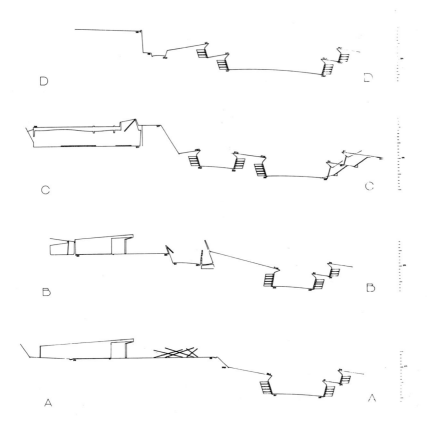

The architects' unwillingness to smooth over breaks in the terrain is linked to the project's assertion of loss as part of corporeality. The treatment of matter also represents this temporality of longer duration. The rusting steel, the worn wood railroad ties, and the vines that will infiltrate the concrete screen walls are spatial expressions of transitory states. Their signs of age index the decomposing bodies that are the unseen subject of the place.

(top left) The loose rock gabion retaining walls in their rusting cages are like threads that stitch the breaks in the earth without attempting to hide them.

(above left) Construction view of tombs in the circular plaza, showing used railroad ties embedded in the ground.

(above) Detail of screen wall with vines, at west side of entry.

(left) Plan and sections of circular plaza showing location of tombs.

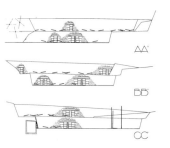

AA'

BB'

CC'

Several strategies prevent the project's many metaphors from becoming sentimental or excessive. One is the tectonic invention that draws them together, fusing the work's bodily sense to its layered siting, to produce a muscular physicality of form. The project also achieves unity by weaving together aggregations of artificial and natural ground, making use of local materials in order to extend the site into the project: the aggregate floor is not, in its materiality, substantively different from the existing soil and rock.

(left) The circular plaza from the second level, with ground tombs in the foreground.

(below left) View of a family tomb facing onto the circular plaza.

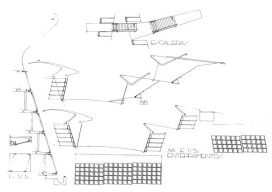

Another strategy uses fragments to open chains of associative meaning that fold metonyms and metaphors into each other, dilating and contracting them across scales to make connections between dissimilar elements. One such chain traces the condition of "embedment" across multiple scales, from the wooden railroad ties in the cemetery floor, to the bodies in the ground, the burial chambers in the hillside, and the section of the mortuary building (not yet built). The architects translate the intensity of this assemblage—where nothing is reduced to background—into spatial terms, where it becomes a locus of interaction between architecture, landscape, and memory. The space is full and empty at the same time, allowing the visitor's attention to circulate across overlapping events and states.

(top) Montjuic Cemetery in Barcelona, showing stone burial-chamber walls in relation to the rocky landscape.

(above) Plan, sections and elevations of burial chamber walls, including stair.

(right) The processional route emerges from the chapel and then reenters the earth, penetrating steeply downward along two flights of concrete stairs. Architecture opens up the ground to create entry for the living as well as the dead: the stair tunnel's bright interior opens outward at the top and bottom of each flight, as if its concrete walls were actively pressing back masses of soil and rock.

The project's powerful incisions and its language of prefabricated concrete produce a tense energy that reverberates between artifice and nature. While the hard-edged burial-chamber walls form a strong contrast with existing topography, their great sloping overhangs establish an almost fluid continuity with the site. Exaggerated scale and sharp-edged abstraction differentiate the cemetery not only from its surroundings, but also from everyday space. This is the realm of the sublime—a space that has the power to move but is not easy to inhabit. Igualada constitutes a breach that cannot be closed or filled, but it also suggests that it is possible to live without the certainty of closure.

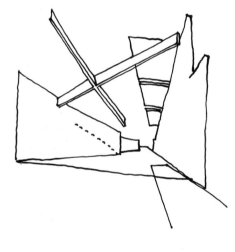

(above) Sketch of temple-crypt as part of processional route that repeatedly introjects visitors into the earth: first through the partially-buried temple-crypt, then through the concrete stairs tunneled between the burial chamber walls.

(above left) The roof of the temple-crypt is pierced by three huge skylights that throw filigreed shadows onto the blank concrete wall.

(left) Visitors can also enter the cemetery to the right of the Cor-ten steel gates, slipping behind a precast concrete screen-wall. The wall, which resembles the cover of the adjoining burial chambers, casts a pattern of shadows onto their bodies, "capturing" them momentarily in a space that evokes the space for corpses within the adjacent wall.

THOMSON FACTORY

Landscape and parking areas
Saint-Quentin-en-Yvelines, France
1991–1992
Desvigne and Dalnoky, Landscape Architects

Desvigne and Dalnoky construe temporality not as transience, but as the ever-changing, which yields an inversion of the traditional association of architecture with permanence and landscape with impermanence. At the Thomson Factory, this inversion serves the program for the site: initially to accommodate a research facility, and eventually to become a park. Advances in research technology make the expected usefulness of the building only several decades, while the landscape is expected to remain permanently. The landscape's permanence, though, is predicated less on specific imagery and more on the expectation of successional change in its material order. Desvigne and Dalnoky deploy the temporal as a mechanism that will enable the radical transformation of the landscape from factory to park. The emphasis on the temporal as an instrument heightens its productive (rather than, say, its phenomenological) aspect: its capacity to construct change, to reform, renew, and reinvent.

Location map. Thomson Factory on the upper right is next to the larger Renault factory.

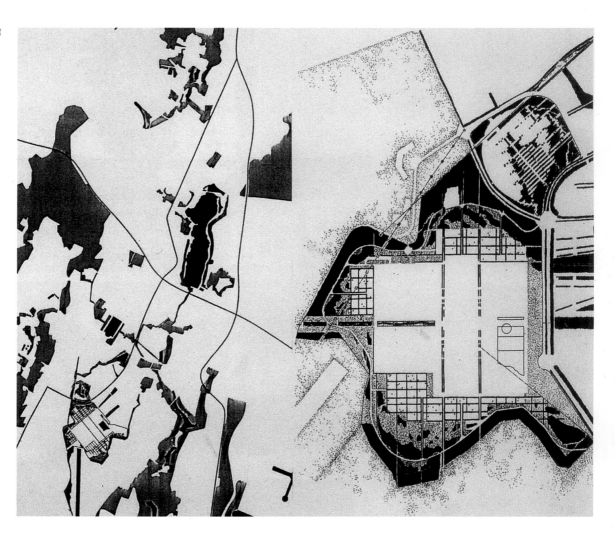

Aerial view of the project. Note landforms on the
periphery, the result of digging the drainage
channels and retention pond.

(above) Views of the retention pond and earthworks on the periphery. The park is a trace, a registration on the site of the processes of its making.

(right) Drainage channel in phase one with initial planting of willow.

The project began as a series of site constructions that prepared the terrain to sustain a building and its construction. The 50–acre (20–hectare) site had impermeable subsoil and no roads or storm drainage. Constructing the ground plane to handle vast amounts of surface water became the essential requirement of the project. Desvigne and Dalnoky folded the surface of the parking lot into multiple channels. Along with other surface channels that collect water from the building's roof, they keep run-off visible throughout the project, rather than forcing it into more traditional underground pipes. This points to the material condition of the soil, its impermeability, and exposes the surface as a construction.

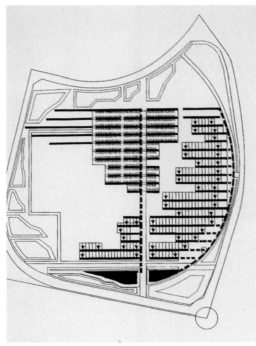

(left) Drainage diagram. Surface runoff would have been increased by the asphalt paving of the 1,000-car parking lot and the roofs of the building. The surface of the parking lot is folded regularly to form drainage channels and collect runoff. The water from the roofs is collected in gutters and also conveyed to surface channels that lead to a filtering device. Once cleansed, the water is stored in a reservoir and recirculated for irrigation.

(below left) Section through parking lot drainage channel.

PLANTATION DE SAULES
SALIX VIMINALIS
SALIX PURPUREA

ROBE   COUVRE SOL : TREFLES   BETON   PARKING

Construction views of parking lot drainage channels. From the outset the building is conceived as the impermanent element of the project, and the landscape as its permanent program.

The initial configuration of the landscape, a field of alternating bands of vegetation, parking lot and channel, is analogous to that of the building. The bands of vegetation begin as lines of willow (*Salix viminalis* and *Salix purpurea*) planted on the banks of the drainage channels to stabilize them. Poplars (*Populus nigra*) are then added to these bands and also planted in thick groves around the perimeter of the site. Conifers (*Pinus sylvestris* and *Pinus nigra*), sweetgum (*Liquidambar styraciflua*) and cedar are planted every consecutive year amongst the poplars. Closer to the building, the scale of the planting responds to the smaller scale of the space, particularly in the interior courtyards. The palette here changes to azalea (*Rhododendron* sp.) and magnolia (*Magnolia* sp.) planted over a ground cover of broom (*Cytisus*). The linear configuration of the planting is continued inside the courtyard, forecasting the eventual removal of the building and the integration of this planting with the planting outside.

After setting up this structure of bands, Desvigne and Dalnoky allow time to begin to construct the landscape. Willow and poplar fix nitrogen in the soil and improve over time its quality as a growing medium. Because they are fast-growing species, they will quickly grow into a forest that is of a scale commensurate with the building's. Meanwhile, the conifers and the hardwoods establish themselves more slowly on the site. Gradually, the poplars and then the willows disappear, their life cycle being shorter than the rest of the species in the park. The initial banded configuration of the landscape will dissolve, through time, into irregular clumps of trees scattered throughout the site, and will constitute the park. The convergence of need and aesthetic posits the temporal aspect of the landscape as both technique of construction and content of the work.

The construction material of the project can be thought of as plant succession itself: the appropriation of the natural life cycle of plants as the system of construction of the park. Evolution and its full disclosure is the subject of the project. As such, the landscape operates as an index, pointing to the very processes of succession that led to its current and evolving state. The building and the landscape are in inverse cycles of similar duration: when the building is no longer useful and is demolished, the landscape will have begun to reach maturity. Through this framework, the landscape suggests a temporality of longer duration than that of architecture.

Parking lot

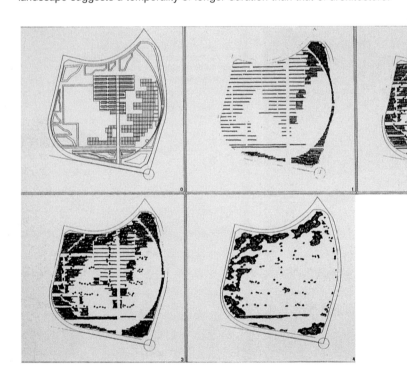

The emphasis on the temporal rejects the possibility that the landscape will achieve one idealized state, which normally leads to static and aestheticized imagery, and accepts the cyclical, the ever-changing, and the unpredictable as the desirable state of the project.

0: Site plan with buildings and parking
1: Phase 1. Creation of a network of drainage channels and their planting with willows. First planting of masses of poplars around the perimeter of the property
2: Phase 2. Additional planting of poplars, of black pine and of isolated clumps of conifers
3: Phase 3. Optimal state of the park of the factory: a field of fast growing poplars, in scale with the plateau surrounds the factory complex
4: Mature state of the park: the slow growing conifers progressively catch up with the poplars. In the end, only the masses of poplars at the perimeter are retained, and the grown specimens provide the main structure of the vegetation.

THRESHOLD

Two concepts are particularly relevant to exploring the operation of threshold. The first, from psychology, defines a threshold as the point at which a stimulus is of sufficient intensity to begin to produce an effect, as in "threshold of consciousness" or "threshold of pain." The second, from ecology, values the edge between two ecosystems as the zone of highest exchange and diversity. In ecological terms, thresholds are the most important parts of a system. The place where field meets forest is more important than either the field or the forest itself.

Thresholds are where transformations begin, where exchanges between unlikely things occur, and where identities are declared. Because they are the result of dynamic relations—between architecture and landscape, public and private, work and recreation—they resist closure in terms of meaning and space. Thresholds hold the potential of an inclusive realm, where the introduction and maintenance of difference is possible. Unlike an idea of inclusion as "melting pot," where identities are blurred to create a compromised whole, threshold as an operation entails the preservation of differences, as well as the creation of something new from their coexistence.

Each project in this section defines and constructs thresholds whose significance as passages is linked to their spatial and experiential semiautonomy from the places and elements they connect. Hierarchy, metonymy, reversal and deferral of passage, and scale, are some of the strategies that may contribute to a threshold's autonomy. At the Villa Cecilia, Torres and Lapeña institute a primary physical threshold that mediates between the worlds of garden and city, and a secondary set of allegorical thresholds that refer to themes of growth and regeneration. Together, these two kinds of thresholds reiterate in the garden a passage between public and private, organic and inorganic, and life and death. The Villa Cecilia also shows how a threshold can stand in metonymically for a whole place. There, the labyrinthine entry to the garden stands between it and the city, as the garden itself stands between city and nature.

An operation of threshold usually functions at more than one scale. In order to effect a transition between spheres of public (street) and private (residence), the landscape architect Catherine Mosbach develops a language of spatial difference for the restoration of the

grounds of the Etienne Dolet housing project. She uses scale to augment the effect of distance between one sphere and another, and extends the domestic outward to unfamiliar scales, thereby bringing forward new readings of urbanity. Hermann Hertzberger's housing also brings the language of the domestic outside, making it possible to inhabit both the public and the private realms simultaneously within the space of the street. The projects demonstrate how the engagement of the domestic with the urban sphere can support new kinds of public space.

The operation of threshold also provides a way to represent the identity of an institution or place in spatial terms, rather than relying on façade or other image-based means. This introductory role is particularly powerful in the Kimbell Museum, where the spatial experience of the bosque of Yaupon trees substitutes for the expected institutional façade. The project externalizes that which has been historically interiorized, that is to say, the garden, displacing it to the front of the building, to perform its most public function. By retaining its interior identity and qualities in spite of its displacement, the threshold-garden of the bosque supports a transition into a different state of mind.

The projects in this section, as well as creating thresholds, represent the idea of threshold. At the Wagner Park, Olin Partnership and Machado Silvetti introduce a condition of distance between a threshold and its occupants that enables them to confront and absorb it from the outside, as object and image, prior to experiencing it spatially. This physical distance induces a contemplative relationship with the threshold artifact that temporarily shifts emphasis and works to delay passage.

Because the operation of threshold hinges on the activity of passage, it inscribes the occupant into the work, in spatial and social terms. Places of encounter and rest that acknowledge the individual are found at the Kimbell Museum and at the Etienne Dolet housing. References that specifically engage the body are found at the Wagner Park (references to eyeball, tear, nostril, and facial hair are present in the threshold's western façade) while at the Villa Cecilia, surrealist-inspired artifacts create an allegory of transformation that both supports and adds dimension to the project's spatial operations.

KIMBELL ART MUSEUM

West Entrance
Fort Worth, Texas, USA
1966–1972
Louis Kahn, Architect

The Kimbell Art Museum's west entrance displaces the association of threshold with margin. Within this threshold space, a double strategy of assertion and negation of both the interior and exterior orders serves to defer entry into the museum and to contribute to the court's spatial and experiential autonomy.

Kahn's siting of the building reasserts the spatial and topographical order of the site. The site, an evenly sloped lawn, had two *allées* of cedar elms (*Ulmus crassifolia*), planted circa 1936, cutting across its entire width, perpendicular to the slope. The building sits at the bottom of this sloped lawn between the street that borders the site and the *allées* of trees. The long dimension of the barrel vaults that form the building is parallel to the allées and contours, continuing the layered structure of the outdoor space. This spatial layering is reinforced by making the main floor of the museum—on the second level of the building and containing the galleries, the bookstore and the cafe—continuous with the entrance court and the lawn. Kahn's insistence on making the main entrance pedestrian, and relegating automobile access to the floor below alongside the less important parts of the program, such as staff offices and bathrooms, further supports the continuity of space between the lawn and the interior of the museum.

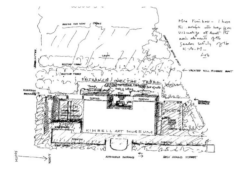

(above) Kahn's sketch, in a letter to Mrs. Kimbell, of his concept for the site plan.

(right) Entrance court from the *allée*.

(bottom) Partial view of south portico, fountain, and bosque

(above) West entrance from the lawn. In the
foreground is one of the two allées of cedar elms.

(right) Site plan.

(bottom) East-west site section, looking north.

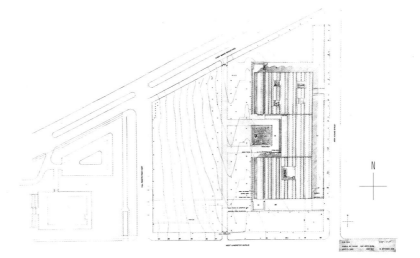

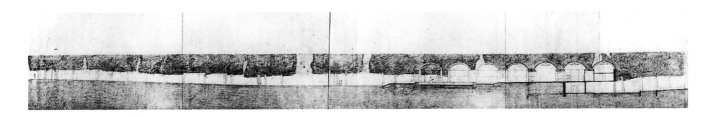

(right) Portico and fountain. The water flows outward from the building toward the lawn, countering the direction of the slope toward the building and delaying spatial change from outside to inside.

(below) Lateral approach to the building from the north. The bosque and its soft ground slow down circulation at the moment of entry.

(bottom) Topographical transitions at the threshold space. Main entry doors to the museum are at right.

However, the spatial continuity that is established between exterior and interior is, on closer inspection, countered at the entrance court. Both the landscape and architectural components of the court—the fountains, the vegetation, and the porticoes—operate at a local scale to disrupt the continuum of the ground plane, circulation, and views.

(right) Views through the densely planted Yaupon bosque toward the lawn.

(bottom) Lateral approach to the building from the south. The end vaults are left open as porticoes, hybrid elements that are as much landscape as architecture.

The siting of a bosque of Yaupon trees (*Ilex vomitoria*) immediately outside the main entrance, and preventing full view of the building from a distance, is the first sign that the threshold is not a space merely to pass through. The trees, densely planted on a 10-foot-by-10-foot (3-meter-by-3-meter) grid, saturate the space of the court. Its geometry, although aligned with the circulation routes, does not respond to any module in the meticulously calibrated building. Both the autonomous geometry of the bosque and its dense spacing have the effect of dispersing vision and movement, ultimately slowing down pedestrian circulation toward the front door just prior to the moment of entry (Benedikt, 1991). To further affirm the entry court's spatial autonomy from both the building and the lawn, Kahn appropriates the existing *allées* as a visual screen to modulate the view outward toward the lawn, contributing to the containment of its space. The lateral approach to the building and the figural strength of the bosque negate the frontality inherent in the symmetrical volumes of the building, and eliminate the wall's potential to function as a façade. The space of the threshold, rather than the image of a façade, is here chosen to represent the institution.

The spatial and metaphorical strength of the entry court is supported by another set of operations that externalize aspects of the interior into the space of the entry court. Like the two interior courtyard gardens, the entry court is an interruption in the iterative field of barrel vaults that comprise the building. It is formed by the removal of two outside vaults from the center bay, producing the building's U-shaped plan. Also like the courtyard garden, the entry court is programmed to invite lingering and accommodate rest, displacing to the outside, to the most public space, those activities that are typically reserved for the private realm of the garden.

Threshold elements: bosque, portico, fountain, and pool.

Finally, to suggest the threshold as a space of inhabitation, the climate in the entry court is modified to mitigate the extreme climate of Fort Worth. Like in the Islamic paradise garden, the deep shade of the bosque, the reflections of water on the underside of the porticoes, and the sound of water cascading to the pools all alleviate the effect of the heat and sun outside. What is typically a place of passage is here presented as refuge itself.

(above) Threshold space as garden.

(left) Fountain, from the portico.

MUNICIPAL OCEAN SWIMMING POOL

Leça de Palmeira, Matushinos, Portugal
1961–1966
Alvaro Siza, Architect

This municipal ocean swimming pool complex sits on an exposed and rocky stretch of the Atlantic coast. The town is a beach destination for the city of Porto, to which it is connected by the Duro River. The project consists of two swimming pools: a rectangular one for adults at the shoreline, and a smaller semicircular one for children adjacent to a protected sand beach. Ramps and walkways connect the pools with sunbathing platforms, a café situated on a large terrace, changing facilities, and the coastal road.

Siza's architecture defines multiple thresholds: between land and sea, constructed and natural, road and beach. His overlay of scales of body, building, and landscape makes it possible both to represent and inhabit this expansive site with its endless horizon and uncontrollable sea. The project engages the regional scale of the rocky coastal landscape, but also represents smaller dimensions of human activity. Its labyrinthine route reproduces the sense of negotiating one's way carefully through the rocks to reach the sea, bringing forward and confirming movements that have existed on the site for generations. The intertwining of new paths and configurations with preexisting ones—both natural and artificial—constructs a landscape layered in time as well as space.

Site plan and site section

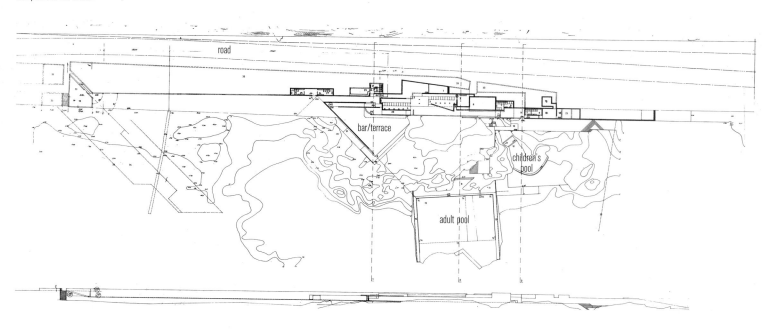

(above) Looking north, with children's pool in foreground and changing rooms at right.

(left) Concept sketch of the intervention as belonging to the layered topography of the coastline.

(above) Looking south; industrial area is beyond.

(right) Looking along the passage to the ocean: the changing rooms are on the left; the ocean is out of view to the right beyond the concrete wall.

The spatial layering of the project reflects the town's long and narrow layout, previously addressed by Siza in his plan for the Marginal, a road along its 5-mile (8-kilometer) coast. Prior to this planning project, an inland road connected the older fishing village at the north end of town, where he had just completed the Boa Nova Tea House, to the less picturesque, industrialized southern portion where the pool is now located. In addition to his sectional strategy of positioning the road more than 20 feet (6.1 meters) above sea level, Siza's planning project had identified the Leça site as one of the few beach spots viable for development along the rocky coast.

The architect transposed his extensive knowledge of the town and the coast into formal, spatial, and material operations of threshold. While a functionally driven solution would merely have made it easier to pass from the road to the ocean, the project multiplies the layers of the site, to make passage through it into a memorable event. His intervention physically restructures the site by cutting into as well as adding to it. Thresholds in section and plan draw the body through the remade landscape, inscribing it into the site, while simultaneously transmitting an idea about the site's structure.

(above) Looking across the children's pool to the beach, beyond at left, and the adult ocean pool, beyond at right.

(below) Looking across the children's pool from under the bridge that connects the changing facilities to the beach.

In this rebuilt environment, architecture relinquishes its conventional identity as autonomous figure, to initiate a dialogue with the striated geology of the natural and industrial landscape. This dialogue begins inland with parallel layers of similarly dimensioned vertical and horizontal surfaces—an architecture that allows itself to be dominated but not eclipsed by the great surface of the sea. These layers become progressively fragmented until the sea finally enters to form the architecture. The project's reductive materiality and muted ochre-grey and blue-green coloration make its figures seem to emerge from the encounter between things that have always been there, as when the undifferentiated expanse of the ocean is drawn into the rock-and-concrete bowl of the adult pool.

(top) Looking from the breakwater across the children's pool to typical highrise development along the coast.

(middle) Pools and beach landscape, seen from the level of the road.

(above) Bar-café and terrace, with bar closed.

(right) Shower and footbath near adult pool.

The project is sited so that the roofs of the concrete building containing the checkroom, changing rooms, toilets, and bar barely rise above the level of the road. This
modest intimation of presence marks the beginning of a journey that heightens the
transformation that occurs between the road and the water's edge, where one eventually arrives in a lightened state of mind and body, having left behind car, clothing,
and other quotidian encumbrances. A final explosive change in register from interior
to exterior is augmented at high tide by the breakwater that with each wave sends a
huge spray up into the air and crashing down into the adult pool, celebrating nature
as uncontrollable, uncontainable process.

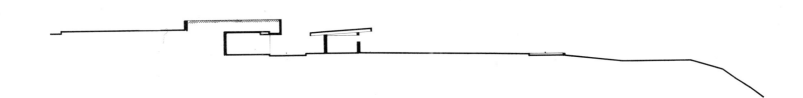

(above) Transverse section showing level changes
from the road, at 25 feet (7.6 meters) above sea
level, to the changing facilities, at 17 feet (5.1
meters), to the ocean pool, at 3.3 feet (1 meter),
to sea level.

(left) The bluish-green copper roof landscape from
the level of the road.

Visitors penetrate the thickness of the linear concrete building in stages, alternating between dark and light, compression and release. As they descend the entry ramp, whose walls angle inward to create a forced perspective, visitors lose sight of the sea along a route where the program is discovered rather than announced. After momentarily passing beneath a roof, the route reaches a checkroom for valuables. It then progresses to the dimly lit changing facilities, from which visitors emerge briefly onto a bright uncovered walkway, where a high wall still delays a view towards the sea. Passing through the showers, they emerge finally onto a bridge, surrounded by animated swimmers and sunbathers, children running back and forth underneath, and the roaring presence and panoramic horizon of the open ocean.

(above) Sand walkway at road level, with amphitheater steps in the foreground.

(right) Wood exterior of women's changing room, illuminated only by natural light entering through gap at the top of the wall.

(above and right) Views of the ocean after emerging from the passage through the building.

HAARLEMMER HOUTTUINEN HOUSING

Amsterdam, Netherlands
1978–1982
Architektuurstudio Herman Hertzberger

The street at Haarlemmer Houttuinen is a place of social contact, a communal living room that supports dialogue between local residents. Within this bracketed urban realm, Hertzberger transforms the concepts of public and private into differentiated spheres of responsibility, using dwelling units as construction material to form the street, making houses and street spatially and programmatically interdependent.

Looking along the narrow residential street, with Hertzberger's building on the right.

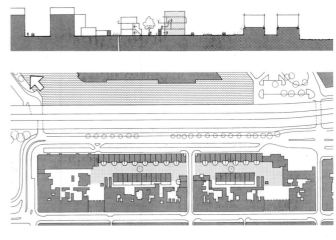

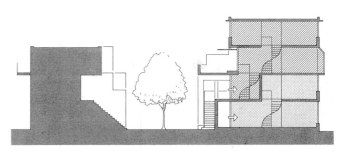

(top) Site section

(above middle) Site plan

(above) Section through street and building.

(left) Exterior, showing balcony.

This mutual consideration of buildings and street is part of an urbanism of everyday spaces, in which to be urban implies being part of a web of interrelationships. For Hertzberger, "the architect is not only a builder of walls, he is also and equally a builder of openings." (Hertzberger, 1983) In this project, he articulates two scales of openings: one between buildings—the narrow street that organizes the project—and one between the inside and the outside of the building itself—the multiple smaller-scale spaces of veranda, balcony, garden, and landing.

This articulation of threshold as a thick zone of events in the region of the building wall divests a front door of its singular significance. Spaces of exchange on both sides of the façade disrupt the conventional alignment of "inside" with "private," and "outside" with "public." However, Hertzberger's intention is to enrich and create a more intimate public realm, rather than to open up a private domain. Actual interpenetration between indoor and outdoor spaces occurs only on the more private upper floors. At street level, the overlap of interior and exterior realms happens outside the weather wall, functioning as suggestions to inhabitants to expand their sphere of operation outward to appropriate the public area as communal space.

The 22-foot-wide (6.7-meter-wide) street recalls the intimate streets in older parts of Amsterdam, where families and neighbors still put out their chairs and tables at tea time. Hertzberger has strategically augmented the street's interior quality by limiting vehicular access, and by disposing trees, lights, bike racks, and gardens in such a way that even a few parked cars make the street impassable to further traffic. This densification of the ground plane is complemented by a similar strategy in the vertical dimension: piers, stairs, and balconies articulate a three-dimensional profile of the street space. Although this is indisputably the front of the project, there is nothing frontal about it; spatially it is suggestive of a more loosely organized backyard realm.

Hertzberger is seeking mechanisms to articulate differences within the public realm. His mandate for neighbors jointly to appropriate their public space challenges a state system that dispenses public works and services from above. His nonmonumental urbanism counters the process through which "city dwellers become outsiders in their own living environment," caught between "not being concerned with the space outside their house nor really [able to] ignore it" (Hertzberger, 1990).

(above) Corner of the building—the rear façade, at left, is not particularly welcoming.

(right) Façade, garden, and street.

The project succeeds in involving residents in a communal realm that is neither residual nor monumental. Yet the fact that it does not engage the city outside its borders calls its publicness into question. If at one scale the articulation of threshold stops at the building's weather wall, it also comes to an abrupt halt at the property line. Hertzberger's intimate public sphere depends on a condition of the local and the familiar, in which strangers would be out of place.

Threshold zone, with lower-unit garden in the foreground.

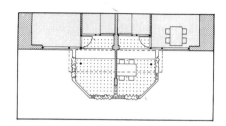

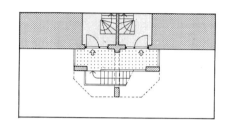

The disposition of units allows direct access to each one from outdoors. There are two types: one-story street-level units and three-story units entered from second-level landings. Projecting piers mark each group of four entrances—two up, two down—and support the third-floor balconies belonging to the upper-unit living rooms. Open steel stairs behind each pier lead to the paired front doors of the larger units, on landings sheltered by the balconies. These stairs in turn protect the lower entries, and provide a space for mailboxes and bicycles.

(top) Unit threshold plans.

(above) The definition between a lower-garden entry and the stair to an upper-unit entry articulates each family's individual responsibility for its outdoor areas.

(right) Threshold zone, showing entries to upper-level units sheltered by living-room balconies.

The many opportunities that the scheme provides for viewing could be experienced as invasive of individual privacy, if it were not for Hertzberger's principle of "adequate but not total separation." His precise disposition and dimensioning of threshold zones of bay windows, balconies, terraces, doorsteps, and porches produces degrees of seclusion. This spatial organization enables an individual in each situation to select a position in relation to others.

Hertzberger's technique of partial definition: balconies are half-roofed, half-exposed; partitions between balconies are lowered to waist height at the front to allow—but not compel—neighborly communication; spaces next to front doors are partially shielded.

VILLA CECILIA

Barcelona, Spain
1983–1986
Jose Antonio Martinez Lapeña & Elias Torres, Architects

This renovation of a walled Renaissance garden in a residential urban neighborhood establishes its identity through the hyperarticulation of the old garden's existing boundary condition. The basis for this reinterpretation has to do with the garden's programmatic transformation from private to public, undertaken during Barcelona's development of public spaces in the 1980s. Rather than minimizing the existing, high boundary wall to create a more open appearance, Torres and Lapeña multiplied and spatialized the boundary as a set of experiences through which the garden discloses an inclusive presence.

The architects exploit the tension between the confined state of the Renaissance garden and the 1980s programmatic shift by throwing attention and energy to the edge: creating a dense series of overlapping layers parallel to the wall at Santa Amelia Street. This strategy of layering plays on the ancient garden figure of the labyrinth. The labyrinth-threshold both represents the garden as a whole and is part of it, metonymically articulating its status as a place between outside and inside, social and natural, civic and intimate.

Axonometric showing hedge-labyrinth at entry.

Aerial view of hedge-labyrinth entry: garden wall
and Santa Amelia Street at left.

The emphasis on its boundary combines with strategies of fragmentation, delay, and framing to obscure perception of the old garden's axially symmetrical organization, which reflected the villa's hierarchical dominance. Now, when the building is encountered comparatively late in the sequence of experience within the layers, it seems to be merely one more slightly surreal garden artifact. Because fragmentation precludes putting the garden back into the whole it once was, the architects are able to use its materials to construct a new sense.

(above) Existing conditions prior to renovation.

(right) Site plan, with Santa Amelia Street at left.

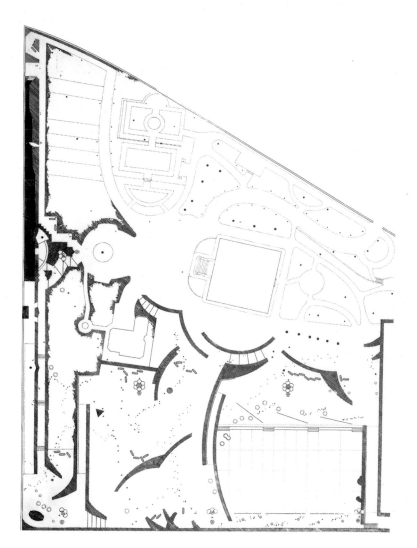

Torres and Lapeña have designed the gates to both the garden and the facing Quinta Amelia Park as events in themselves, appropriating the street as an ambiguous quasi-garden realm. They have also intensively colonized the space of the wide sidewalk in front with trees, hedges, and flowers, as if this lush vegetation, unable to be contained, had spilled over the high wall.

(top) Looking from the gates of Quinta Amelia Park toward the entry to Villa Cecilia, across Santa Amelia Street.

(above) When closed, the gates to the garden leave behind small fragments on the wall, as if they had rusted permanently open.

(above left) The Villa Cecilia gates open; the fanning metal, leaflike layers spell the name of the garden and suggest a flattened labyrinth.

(left) Elevations of entrance gates open and closed.

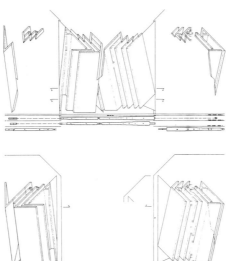

(top) Looking east—back toward the entry—at the far end of the moat, with the garden wall at right.

(middle) Within the labyrinth, a small "tongue" of concrete signals the presence of a tiny platform on the other side of the hedge, overlooking the moat.

(bottom) Looking through a hedge to the sculpture of a drowned woman, one of numerous localized tableaux that appropriate the existing wall as a part of the labyrinth.

(right) In the second layer of the labyrinth, a re-encounter with the gingko pergola sponsors a look back through the entry gate to the parklike street, at right.

Numerous localized events occur within the boundary space of the labyrinth entry. The wall itself is inscribed by the gates, clasped at the top by metal gingko leaves. Wires that look like hair grow out of it into the moat. The architects introduce additional motifs along this folding green corridor: small cuts in the hedge allow transgression into intimate spaces for reflection. These interconnections between layers act as counterpoint to the typically impassable condition of the hedge.

On passing through the ivy gates, visitors find themselves on a gravel path within a hedge of tall asymmetrically clipped cypress. By blocking direct visual and physical passage forward from the entry, this hedge deflects attention to the two sides. To the left, a moat emerges from beneath the ground plane on which the visitor stands. Turning right to proceed laterally, the visitor immediately encounters a large sycamore tree (*Platanus orientalis*) occupying the middle of the path.

(above) Moat at the left of the entry, which extends to the end of the garden, forming a reflective corridor. It is inhabited by a sculpture of a drowned woman, and framed by a pergola of huge metal gingko leaves.

(left) At the entry to the garden labyrinth, looking east toward a sycamore tree (*Platanus orientalis*) in the center of the path, with the entry gate at right.

As well as constructing thresholds between city and nature, Torres and Lapeña displace the boundaries between states of being—life and death, growth and decay, real and unreal—to create a surreal poetics of unstable identities. The flattened-ivy gate, the metal-leafed pergola, the hairy wall, and the rebellious tree belong to this other kind of threshold—a region of metamorphosis in which a hedge is architecture, and art is becoming-vegetal; a tree asserts its sculptural identity, and "lampelunas" light fixtures like giant water lilies, wave high in the air next to the palm trees.

The combination of techniques of fragmentation and inversion narrows the conceptual distance between city and nature, shifting the garden's identity from one defined in terms of this opposition, to an artifactual realm where everything, including the villa, is a fragment displaced from another time or space. The distancing of artifacts from their preconceived categories of identity sets up an oscillating field of relationships.

(above) Lampeluna

(right) Garden interior, showing white concrete "lines," embedded in the surface of the hard-packed earth, that articulate changes in level, as if the entire garden was a life-size topographical map.

(above) Outside the Villa Cecilia, with shadows
of planting on the wall, and planting in the
garden beyond.

(left) Hide-and-seek in the labyrinth.

Reinterpreting the villa's boundary as a threshold calls into question the conventional
meanings of both garden and city. Because the bounded garden as a type has not
been a part of the modern public realm, it offers a possibility now to elude established constraints. By valuing the historical role of the wall as a limit, instead of deny-
ing it, the architects give the garden a paradoxical, articulate identity as urban space.

ETIENNE DOLET PUBLIC HOUSING

outdoor spaces
Issy-les Moulineaux, France
1990–1992
Catherine Mosbach, Landscape Architect

This rehabilitation of outdoor spaces in a multifamily housing complex in a suburb of Paris redefines the transition between city and home as an urban-domestic realm that is part belvedere and part backyard. Mosbach, who has commented that "the smoothing over of public space is unbearable,"(Mosbach, 1995) resists a transparent universalizing exteriority by placing equal emphasis on different elements and scales of relationships.

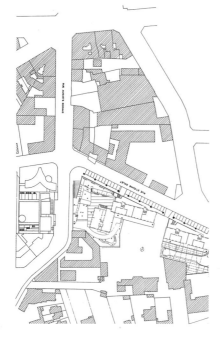

(above) Site plan

(right) Site plan of intervention

(below) Site plan prior to intervention

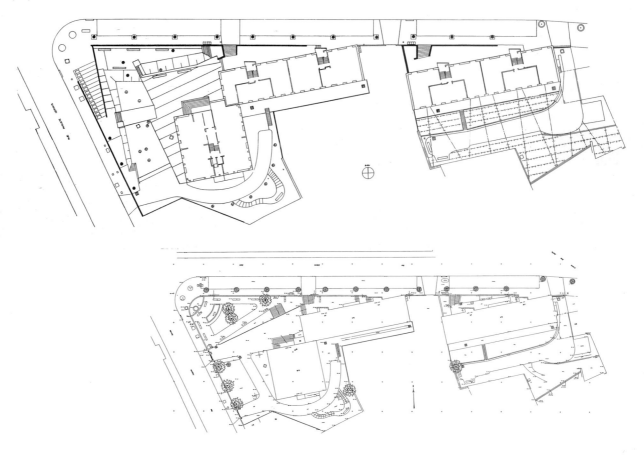

(above) Looking south up the wood stair ramp
that is the principal entry to the square, with a
forced-perspective focus on the chestnut tree at
the top.

The landscape architect describes her project as born out of the ambiguous status of the place. Prior to her intervention, architecture, landscape, and city existed on the site as if in parallel, unconnected universes: a ten-story tower block was entered through a run-down garden on a 13-foot-high (4-meter-high) concrete base; the base dominated the space of the sidewalk without participating in it. With modest means Mosbach has recast the place as a landscape of connections: constructing new relations between these disjunctive realities without attempting to unify them. Her actions include cladding the surfaces of the concrete base, reterracing and resurfacing the land—while preserving six mature chestnut trees (*Castanea sativa*)—and redirecting movement to the tower entry by way of the reconfigured garden.

Elevation along Rue Auguste Gervais, showing the relationship of the intervention to the building.

Mosbach's project inscribes the previously inarticulate concrete base with multiple events that enable passage and construct opportunities for viewing and inhabitation. She erodes the barrier effect of the base by shifting the main entrance to the intersection of the two main streets. At this corner, a wooden stair-ramp connects the levels of street and garden, its forced perspective focusing attention on a large chestnut tree that visually fills the narrow space at the top. The specificity of this moment of arrival (at the tree), at which there is a view north to the city of Paris, acts as a cipher for the project, signaling a reworking of relations between culture and nature, distance and intimacy. Following this arrival, lines of movement break down into small eddies and knots within the garden that encourage individual encounters. The overlay of elements of different sizes and from different historical moments supports an abstraction that is grounded in its material context.

(top) The wood screen wall regulates the difference in level between the Rue August Gervais that slopes toward downtown, and the garden that descends in landings.

(above) Looking south within the garden; existing chestnut trees become a point of arrival.

(left) Existing chestnut trees at the top of the entry stairs, looking north; the wood landings organize the garden and make it possible to avoid building collars around the trees. Compare this view with the previous conditions below.

(below left) Looking north toward Paris, prior to Mosbach's intervention, showing three existing chestnut trees and the poverty of the relationship between the sidewalk and the residential square.

Mosbach constructs a threshold realm that is simultaneously open and closed, by implementing the disparity in level between street and garden. Originally seen as a negative characteristic, this disparity makes it possible to limit places of transition from public to semipublic without resorting to fences, which would more explicitly signify closure. At a finer grain, the development of the different levels of ground within the garden organizes it visually and spatially, taking an individual's shifting position into account.

(above) Looking west in the garden with belvedere to Rue Etienne Dolet; south-facing benches encircle the existing chestnut trees.

(right) Looking east at the relationship between the high garden under the boughs of the chestnut trees and Rue Etienne Dolet below, with parking.

(bottom right) Looking southwest from small court at tower entry, toward ash and linden trees.

The project's extensive use of wood, a material typically associated in Europe with domestic interiors, crosses the traditional dichotomy between public-urban and private-domestic realms. Wood also provides a material consistency that affects the perception of the precinct from the city beyond. The wood cladding of the base is explicitly not an attempt to mask its size—a wall along one of the stairs remains high even as the terrain drops. The semitransparent pattern of this wall defines the space of the garden without sealing it off. Mosbach also uses wood to represent other scales within the garden that are more likely to be associated with backyards, accommodating level changes and surface treatments with an apparent casualness.

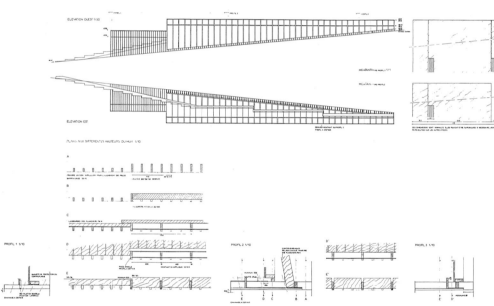

(above) Looking west along the wood walkway at the garden perimeter: the narrow footpath slips behind a bench as it negotiates changes in level; a small wood platform embedded in the ground beneath one of the chestnut trees suggests an intimate space, scaled to an individual body. The eighteenth-century building beyond will become a museum of garden plans.

(left) West elevation of wall (top); east elevation of wall; plan details; views of wall at different heights.

(below left) Detail, beginning of wood screen.

Wood also represents a condition that is less permanent and more fragile than the concrete it covers. This representation of fragility challenges the myth of low maintenance in public housing that produces the dilapidated conditions such as those that characterized this project prior to its renovation. The purposeful use of a material that requires looking after integrates this requirement into the conceptual base of the project.

On the sidewalk of Rue Etienne Dolet looking west, showing the relationship between the new wood cladding and the existing wall. As a result of this rehabilitation, the town has decided to enlarge the sidewalk and change the direction of parking, to privilege pedestrian passage.

Mosbach's intensification of the effects of scale and distance supports the development of a language of spatial difference, which she uses to critique modern architecture and urbanism's suppression of domesticity and nature. By extending the intimacy of a domestic scale outward to different scales of relationships, she brings forth new readings of urbanity as well as domesticity. Her approach engages the urban but at the same time resists monumentality by enlarging the sphere of the previously passed-over, and overlaying it onto the preexisting spaces of the city.

(top) View from the intersection of Augustus Gervais and Etienne Dalet, with tower block at left.

(above) On the sidewalk of Rue Etienne Dolet, looking west, showing the cladding of the wall with wood veneer at the higher level, by the guard house, and with planks below.

(left) Visual progression of the stair-ramp toward chestnut trees.

ROBERT F. WAGNER, JR. PARK

New York, New York, USA
1993–1996
Machado and Silvetti Associates, Inc.
Olin Partnership, Landscape Architects

Threshold in the Robert F. Wagner Jr. Park acquires different configurations as a result of the site's location between the vast landscape of the New York harbor to the west, and the monumental city to the east. To mediate between these shifts in scale, Olin Partnership conceived the park as a series of thresholds between city and harbor, each one responding to specific spatial and programmatic conditions of its immediate context.

(right) From the river, the building seems a fragment of a previously colossal structure like the buildings of Wall Street behind it.

(below right) The park, looking toward the Hudson River.

(below) Location plan.

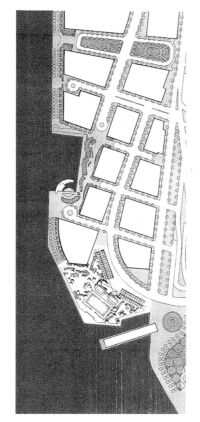

(above) Perspective view of park building from waterfront.

(left) Site plan.

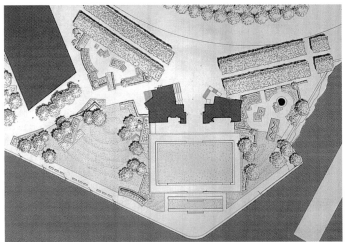

The partially dissolved edge of the park's western side enables the inclusion of the harbor into the space of the park. More specifically, it allows the project to be identified with the Statue of Liberty, the building to be construed as the temple from which she emerged, and the landscape as her ancient garden in ruin. Threshold along West Street is, in marked contrast, a series of events layered along the street edge. The first layer is formed by double *allées* of red maple (*Acer rubrum*) that direct movement toward the park's main entrance plaza, conceived as a place for public events and performances. The following layer, a building flanked by gardens, is programmed to defer and possibly preclude passage, countering the function of the threshold as a place of transition by presenting itself as destination. The gardens' strong figural presence, derived from their geometric configuration, their plant material, and their sunken ground planes, as well as their program as places for rest, disengages them from an association with passage. The building's character changes dramatically from one side to the other, reflecting its multiple roles as boundary, passage and destination.

(top) At the end of each allée, a view of the monumental stairs does not disclose their destination. Parallel to the sidewalk and directly adjacent to it, this apparent redundancy reveals a desire to stage arrival to the park and to present the threshold as an artifact to be contemplated from a distance.

(middle) Gardens at the threshold, showing shifting horizon lines at flower beds.

(above) The park, looking south; sculpture by Jim Dine.

(right) From the harbor side the park appears as if in the process of decay, its flower beds strewn throughout the lawn, tilting, partly buried, as if dislodged from their initial position.

The building's east façade is almost exclusively concerned with threshold and its representation. It is, in effect, a monumental portal that frames the view to the Statue of Liberty. The view through the portal is the only moment of singular significance in the park, where the main threshold to the park is explicitly identified with threshold to the nation. The architects use a sectional strategy to appropriate the statue and its context into the park. The ground rises within the portal to an elevated grass terrace at the water side of the building. The higher elevation of this terrace conceals the esplanade and its rail at the water's edge, giving the impression that the plane of grass is coplanar and continuous with the water, foreshortening the distance between the statue and the site. Passage is also thematized at both sides of the portal, where steps, bleachers, and platforms—elements that denote and provide spatial transitions—form the façade of the building.

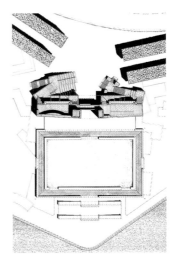

(above) Site plan showing *allées*, park building and lawn terrace.

(below) Building's east façade, with view of Statue of Liberty framed by the portal. The architects visually foreshortened the distance from the portal to the statue by manipulating the ground plane between the building and the water. The removal of the lamp posts that are typically integrated with the rail at the esplanade further exaggerates the compression of distance.

In fact, the visitors are never led to the interior of the building. The stairs lead to other stairs, then momentarily to a platform, then to other stairs, and then to terraces and the bridge on the building's roof, where visitors can sit with their backs to the city, and revisit the view seen from the portal, this time presented in a panorama. Visitors are not expected to enter the building: it houses park maintenance equipment, bathrooms, and a café. The places of habitation are the building's outside surfaces. What was presented from the west as a pavilionlike building amidst a vast landscape for quiet relaxation and contemplation is here transformed into a building with exterior surfaces that accommodate and support civic life.

(top) The walls at the ramps that make the transition form the terrace to the esplanade are dimensional and detailed to accommodate and/or refer to the body. The sculpture is by Louise Bourgeois.

(above) North stairs

(right) Stairs and bridge connect the two sides of the building at rooftop level. This vertical landscape also serves to keep visitors in transition within the threshold space, while in a promenade to a climactic view.

Once through the portal, the one-to-one relationship of visitors with the statue is dispersed, and other choices of views and events—flower beds, shady groves of Goldenraintree (*Koelreuteria paniculata*), solitary benches, walls for reclining and sunbathing—are presented. The public subject inscribed on the street side of the building is here transformed into a private, contemplative individual. A secondary set of references to the body—to eyeball, eyebrow, tear, facial hair—on the river façade of the building, as well as the figurative sculptures by Louise Bourgoise and Jim Dine, further support the inscription of the individual in the park.

Olin's landscape and Machado and Silvetti's architecture transform the threshold into spaces for recreation and for contemplation. By conflating these multiple uses and codes of meaning the idea of threshold is made ambivalent, both inviting and negating passage in order to create place.

(above) Looking south from the north stair. The east façade's steps, bleachers, and platforms accommodate visitors watching performances on the plaza. To the left is the double *allée* of red maple.

INSERTION

Insertion initiates cycles of activity and reactivity between an existing urban context and a new, inserted, space. This operation stands against the modernist notion of undifferentiated open space, and also rejects historicized contextualism, in which new architectural and landscape architectural projects are designed to blend in seamlessly with their surroundings.

Insertion engages a space with its surroundings, such that it becomes part of an urban continuum, but also initiates a break in that continuum. The interface between the space and its context is not smooth or invisible: insertion depends on activating boundaries to construct identity. Part of a space's identity is its relations with surrounding spaces. Its edges define a space as different from but also related to the spaces around it. As one space is introduced into another it comes into transformative, sometimes uncomfortable, contact with existing orders. Insertion can operate by importing something foreign into a site, or by foregrounding some quality that was already present but not apparent.

The insertion of a space into the city, which is the subject of this chapter, is different from the insertion of an autonomous object, such as a monument. A monument "denotices" its surroundings by rising above them, and transforming them into passive receivers. While monuments are characterized by the solidity of their boundaries, a space can "notice" its environment through the careful configuration of its boundaries.

Insertion initiates a relationship of interdependency between a space and its context. In the Plaça del General Moragues in Barcelona, Olga Tarrasó embraces a context by "reprocessing" its ordinary materials, such as brick and granite, in spatial and constructional terms. Similarly, at the Jacob Javits Plaza in New York, Martha Schwartz uses traditional New York City Parks Department materials but deforms them, juxtaposing them in their new state against the adjacent context.

Insertion can also engage temporal aspects by exposing previous urban layers, in order to reveal continuities and disjunctions between past and present. In the Fossar de les Moreres in Barcelona, Carmen Fiol uses excavation to expose events in the history of the site that allow her to represent it in social terms. These conditions of temporal and spatial interdependency tend to operate primarily at a local scale. Unlike monuments, these spaces are not visible from a distance.

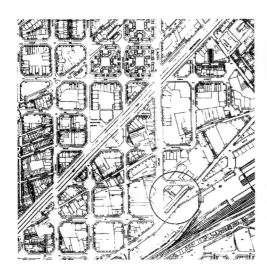

Both of the Barcelona projects were part of the city's urban redevelopment in the 1980s. One radical aspect of this undertaking was its emphasis on "projects not planning." Equally radical was that outdoor spaces, rather than buildings, became the basis for the reconstruction of the city. Providing outdoor space as a network of independent places, rather than as a conventional, large, objectifiable expanse of parkland, demonstrates the operation of insertion at an urban scale: discreet interventions are scattered throughout the city, each one engaging its immediate context in specific and singular ways. Detailed analysis of the city at different scales was a critical aspect of Barcelona's urban makeover, one that served to avoid the dangers of abstraction inherent in master planning.

The other two projects in this section are located in Manhattan, both on platforms of "artificial" ground, a common site condition in contemporary cities. Dan Graham's installation "Two-way Mirror Cylinder Inside Cube and Video Café" is on the roof of the Dia Foundation, a four-story loft building at the western edge of the city. Martha Schwartz's Jacob Javits Plaza is at street level above an underground parking lot, surrounded by large federal and local government buildings. These two projects represent a mode of insertion that inverts categories: both "turn city into landscape." Whereas Schwartz inverts the meaning of the place itself through the physical manipulation of materials, Graham's installation transforms the Dia Center's urban surroundings into a landscape, by allowing the spectator visually to reapprehend this context.

Each of these projects functions as a "not object" to subvert normative expectations and reconfigure its surroundings. All of them work against monumentality to construct relations of exchange between the new and the existing. The value of this operation rests in the critical potential of these relations in the making of urban social space.

PLAÇA DEL GENERAL MORAGUES

Barcelona, Spain
1986–1988
Olga Tarrasó, Architect

This public space is located in an industrial-residential fringe of Barcelona, where two of the three streets that border its triangular perimeter are part of the city's metropolitan traffic network. Three composite planes of different materials, textures, inclinations, and colors each mark a particular territory within this constructed urban landscape. A new triangle, superimposed upon the first, is buffered from the busy urban perimeter by the play of the three planes linking them. However, the inner triangle is the least-developed part of the small park. It is the three margins that become memorable urban places.

Tarrasó does not attempt to overcome the site's condition of marginality by positing a new monumental presence or a powerful centralizing figure. Rather, she has made an architecture of seams, where each seam marks an encounter between urban orders. This strategy addresses diverse needs of function and urban identity. Each margin sets the stage for differing activities and yet, owing to the care given to the joints between them, they form a cohesive landscape.

Surfaces coming together at the northwest entry to the park.

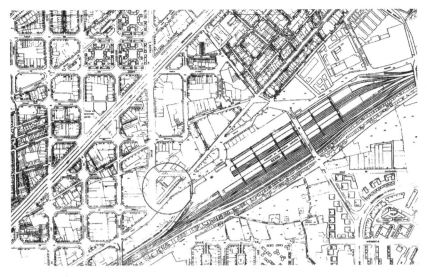

(top) Location plan of existing conditions prior to Tarrasó's intervention, 1986, showing the relationship of the site to major traffic arteries.

(middle) Detail of seam between concrete steps and brick hill at northwest entry.

(bottom) Model, from above

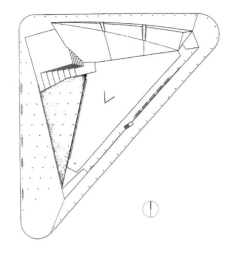

This strategy of seams operates both within the park and in relation to its context. Each margin works to integrate the park with—or withstand—the many scales of activity beyond its physical borders. At the same time, each one adjusts to meet and support the empty center of crushed gravel; each is a place from which to observe and participate in spaces within and outside the park. Their sectional configuration supports complex open boundaries without the use of walls or fences: raising the park's ground planes differentiates it from the city, and shifts the horizon from within.

(top) Plan

(above) Sidewalk at the north side of the park, showing the changing slope of the brick terrain.

(right) Looking south across the newly-constructed plaza from the brick hill. Soccer game in the center of the park, using an Ellsworth Kelly sculpture as the goal; the two monumental sculptures were originally commissioned for another public space.

Along the short western side of the park, a generously widened sidewalk lined with benches connects the pedestrian flow to and from the bridge across nearby railroad tracks that divide northern and southern sections of the city. A grid of trees that begins on the sidewalk continues across the break in section that marks the boundary of the park onto the raised, level lawn, creating a strong visual relationship between exterior and interior. This double operation uses a sectional strategy to separate and a plan strategy (of the tree grid) to stitch together, in order to accommodate the differing grain, scale, and program of the exterior and interior spaces. The east-west-grained, inward-facing lawn is a space of stillness, in contrast to the north-south-grained sidewalk, which is broad enough to accommodate the movement of crowds, while providing a moment of shade.

(above) Bench at the inner edge of the west margin.

(left) Benches at the edge of the wide sidewalk with the grid of trees, at the west side of the park. Bridge to the south is by Santiago Calatrava, 1986.

(below left) West margin, looking from the interior. The tree grid continues from the raised lawn to the concrete sidewalk.

(top) Outer (at left) and inner (at right) edges of brick terrain at the north margin, looking east, showing relationship to the center.

(right) View of brick terrain at the northwest corner entry to the park.

(below) Diagrammatic construction drawings of brick hill, with spot elevations.

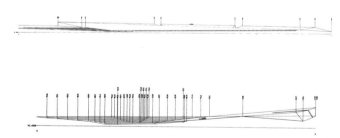

A south-facing inclined plane of brick occupies, with shifting topography, the least-trafficked north side of the park. It is broken at intervals with ramped entries that cut into the side of the hill. While it presents an almost vertical face to the sidewalk, as it folds over into the park, the hill shifts scale and gains a figural identity as a land-scape. This shift allows it to compete with the large scale of the surrounding housing projects in a way that it could not if it were merely a continuous flat surface. As topography that is simultaneously surface and mass, it is able both to gather its surroundings and to make a memorable landmark out of ordinary urban materials.

The southern margin is simultaneously directed inward by the orientation of its benches and railings, and outward by its material continuity with the concrete sidewalk and the transparency of its railing-seat assembly. A technique of overlapping negotiates tensions between inside and outside: the concrete ground plane begins as a narrow strip at the east entry and progressively thickens in plan and section; when it reaches an inhabitable dimension, a railing is added; after the railing establishes its rhythm, a bench is added, which uses the railing as its back; then trees are added; as soon as the space has gained its full complement of urban furnishings, they are interrupted to allow a fragment of the ground plane to peel away into a midblock stairway.

The plaza supports the possibility of collective life through its modes of operation, rather than by representing a civic identity through forms or images. It works because attention is paid to encounters and clashes, countering the way in which they are ignored in the context, or suppressed in more hierarchically ordered public spaces. Its urbanity comes from the way that relationships between and across scales are not only facilitated but also represented. It affirms its disparate context by making evident the potential of marginal places to support heterogeneity.

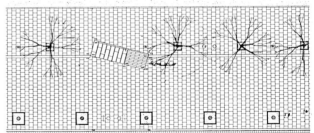

(top) South margin at the western end, showing the ramped entry.

(middle) South margin at the eastern end of the park, showing the grade change at the sidewalk, at left, and the ramped entry leading to the center of the park, at right.

(above) Plan detail and diagrammatic elevation of the stair that connects the sidewalk and the south margin of the park.

(left) South margin seen from the sidewalk level, showing the railing and beginning of the bench.

FOSSAR DE LES MORERES

Barcelona, Spain
1989
Carmé Fiol, Architect

This tiny rectangular brick plaza in the historic center of Barcelona has the quality of an urban room. Insertion, in this case, began with the demolition of residential buildings occupying the site, as part of an attempt to revitalize this dense, medieval part of the city. It is a paradoxical space that unsentimentally inserts the past into the present; it has been made more full by being emptied out, and its expressive moments have to do both with events long past and those just passing through.

When historical research revealed that the site had been a mass grave for victims of Catalonia's war of independence, the architect's goal was to enable the everyday use of the small square, but also to create a symbolic space, which would resonate with past events. Its memorial identity is inscribed in the name of the project, *fossar* being a Catalan word that means mass grave.

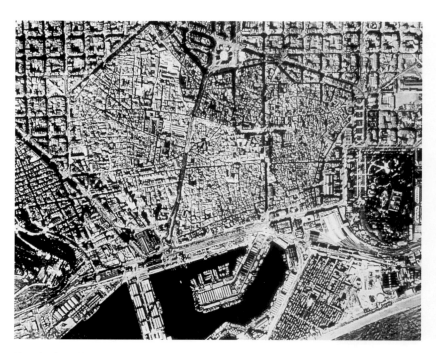

(above) Aerial view of dense urban fabric surrounding the plaza.

(left) Site conditions, 1983, prior to demolition.

The plaza retains the outline of the footprint of the buildings that were demolished to create it, emphasizing the center of the site—the memorial—as a virtual interior. This interiority is supported by the high silent church wall that, in combination with the dimensional traces of the tiny houses, gives a strange scale to the plaza, making it seem simultaneously intimate and grand. At the same time, the notion of a safe or conventional interiority is subverted by the inward-sloping topography within the outline of the footprint, that suggests going beneath the ground, in memory of the heroes who were buried there.

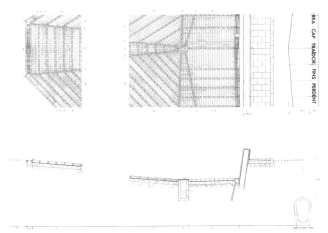

(above) Looking from Callé Malcuinat to the interior of the memorial space.

(top right) The sloping ground plane from within the space.

(middle right) Looking north, along the stone tablet: the ground plane of the center descends to meet the elevation occupied by the mass grave, at the center of the red granite wall.

(right) Detail plans and sections showing paving and drainage channels, a primary focus of the careful detailing of the project.

(clockwise from top)
Drawing of the memorial granite tablet.

The granite tablet with church façade above, showing layering.

The square and the tilted granite wall, from Callé Santa Maria.

Northeast corner of piazza, at sitting area beneath mulberry trees (*moreres*).

Looking west, across the memorial space and the granite wall, with Callé Santa Maria beyond.

A polished dark red granite tablet that forms a low wall along the northwest side of the square is inscribed with an epitaph "to the martyrs of 1714: in the Fossar de les Moreres no traitor is buried; even if we lose our flags it will be the urn of honor." The color of the granite refers to the blood of heroes that saturated the square in 1714. The wall's slight tilt both references a lack of solidity to the ground below, and discourages its use as a seat. Like the sloping ground plane, the wall's simultaneous modesty and resistance to easy occupation contribute to the austere quality of the space.

The architect (and her partner Andreu Arriola) have previously stated "[I]n this park we will never plant a tree." The idea that the space would harbor no living thing was part of a strategy to create a present emptiness that would heighten the fullness of an absent past. However, a small grove of trees planted in one corner of the outer part of the space continues a process of layering of present and past, living and dead, that is what constitutes history.

As well as connoting an interior, the inscription of the footprint of the demolished buildings traces and preserves the narrow walkways that once circulated around the houses. These walkways connect with a larger network of urban movements that now seem to meet in the plaza, emphasizing its identity as a clearing in the forestlike density of this medieval part of the city. While open to this network of everyday life, the square's geometry, topography, and carefully configured boundaries give it a sense of being apart from its surroundings, and prevent it from being overwhelmed by the movement across and beside it. The Callé Malcuinat, a tiny street leading from the Plaça del Palau, enters the plaza at the center of the side opposite from the church. Its potential to bisect and fragment this small space is diffused through the differentiation of the plaza into inside and outside. On the other side of the square, the low height of the granite wall precludes its being perceived as a barrier, and allows activity of different scales to animate the emptied-out space from beyond its borders.

(left) West corner of piazza, looking toward the side entrance to Santa Maria del Mar: maintaining the paving of the narrow perimeter walkway in the typical sandstone cobbles emphasizes this part of the site as an exterior, in contradistinction to the brick-lined center of the space.

(below left) The square from the side entry of Santa Maria del Mar.

TWO-WAY MIRROR CYLINDER INSIDE CUBE AND VIDEO CAFÉ

Rooftop Installation at the Dia Center for the Arts
New York, New York, USA
1991
Dan Graham, Artist
Baratloo-Balch Architects

The project is a glass-enclosed square wooden platform, raised several feet above the level of the roof of the Dia Center. Visitors access the platform up a small flight of stairs, and then have the option to proceed into an cylindrical inner court, also wrapped by a glass skin, through a pivot door. When closed, the door is barely noticeable. Opening it breaks the surface of the cylinder, and draws the emphasis from the surrounding space of the platform inward, setting up an oscillation of focus between the two elements—the cube and the cylinder—each of which is simultaneously a space and an object.

This shifting focus between space and object is one of numerous oscillations that Graham sets up, which sustain tensions between the group and the individual, place and displacement, solidity and transparency, city and landscape, interior and exterior, permanent and temporary, architecture and art. These multiple oscillations interact to construct a paradoxical space.

(above) Within the cube, with pivot door open.

(below) Looking across the pavilion to the water tower.

(above) View of the cylinder through the outer
layer of glass.

(left) Detail of pivot door in open position.

The glass produces a condition that alternates between seeing and being seen, transparency and self-observation. This emphasis on unstable images continues Graham's ongoing research into the vulnerability of visual perception to different kinds of mediation, including video. Here, the physical positioning of viewer-participants recasts the city as "landscape." Elevating the ground plane above the spatial volume of the roof, as defined by the parapet, avoids a sense of visual and physical enclosure. It also eliminates the distraction of paraphernalia such as skylights and mechanical equipment, enabling Graham to project the pavilion's spatial field out into the larger urban landscape.

(top) Within the cylinder.

(above) Cityscape from within the cylinder.

(right) The cylinder and the water tower, with the photographer-artist reflected in the cube.

At first, the pavilion appears to be an object in the high modern tradition, pristinely aloof from its urban industrial surroundings. Yet its hard-edged steel-and-glass materiality also allows it to be absorbed into its surroundings. Its subject is these surroundings, reflected in its glass surfaces and reproduced in its materials and dimensions. Sources for these materials and dimensions are visible in the piers along the Hudson River, in the cage for active recreation on the roof of the neighboring women's detention center, and the water tower on the Dia Foundation roof.

The artist chose the roof as a site when he was invited to make a temporary installation at the Dia Foundation. He involved the architects Baratloo and Balch to help address the construction of the project, which was complicated by the need to make it demountable, since it was commissioned—more than six years ago—as a three-year installation. To achieve the cantilever of the outer bays, and to avoid overloading the structural capacity of the roof, a truss brings loads directly onto two existing columns in the four-story loft building. Graham and the architects also worked to integrate structural with glass-mounting requirements, to maintain a thin profile.

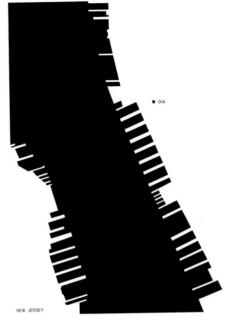

NEW JERSEY

(above) Location plan

(left) Looking from the Dia Foundation roof to the women's detention center, showing the recreation cage on its roof.

(bottom left) Section of building with installation at the top.

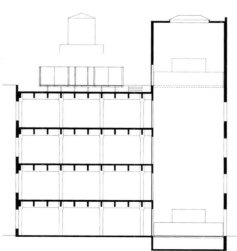

(above) Within the cube, with pivot door of cylinder closed.

(below) The three spaces—cylinder, cube, and roof—occupied at a Dia Foundation event.

Is the project a temple? A garden? A viewing apparatus? An environment to inhabit? A performance space? Graham situates it in a hybrid iconographic lineage that includes the primitive hut, theorized by Abbé Laugier as architecture's supposed origin, Mies van der Rohe's and Philip Johnson's glass houses, and the mass-produced domesticity of suburban tract houses. The piece cannot really sustain all these metaphorical relationships. Yet its success has to do with the resonance between its metaphorical references and the metonymic activity through which it engages its physical context.

The artist's definition of the pavilion as a "small public park" is, at best, wishful think-ing, since it is accessible only through the lobby, elevator, and halls of its elite institutional sponsor. However, the pavilion does call into question the common equa-tion of interiority with privacy. Notwithstanding its exposed position, it produces the sense of an interior, that is augmented by the double passage inward through two glass skins. Yet to occupy the most interior volume is to be the most on display.

Although the pavilion cannot will itself to be a public space, it does have the capacity to become different things for different people. As well, the strength of its boundaries allows it to articulate a space that it can give back to the city around it. These characteristics combined with the conjunction that it produces between art and everyday space are the ingredients of a successful public place, were it to be located in a space that was publicly accessible.

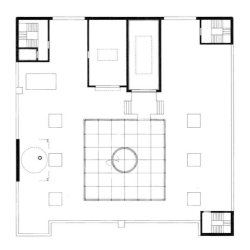

(top) Plan of installation and building roof: the platform is made up of thirty-six steel-framed 6-foot-square (1.8-meter-square) bays; twenty are cantilevered, making the platform appear to float.

(above) Aerial view of the pavilion.

JACOB JAVITS PLAZA

New York, New York, USA
1995–1996
Martha Schwartz, Inc.

At the Javits Plaza, relations between the plaza and its context are activated through a strategy of inversion, in which materials not typically associated with landscape—such as urban furnishings—become landscape. This functional inversion, in which, for example, benches are rendered as landscape and grass as freestanding object, is Schwartz's critique of natural-looking scenery as the unquestioned paradigm for the design of public space in New York City. Paradoxically, Schwartz did not reject the standard program for New York City plazas: to provide passive recreation for workers during their lunch hour within a space that was primarily green.

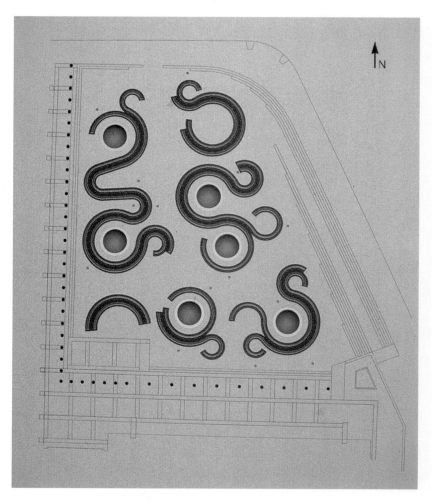

Site plan

(above) Looking toward the sycamore trees of the Thomas Payne Park across the street.

(right) The program—seating and contemplation— is exploded to become the sole material and metaphorical content of the plaza. Schwartz empties the landscape elements' traditional content and replenishes them with new ones.

(top) The grass mounds sporadically spew steam out of their tops. On these occasions, the grass is further transformed from its typical role of background surface to freestanding object and fountain.

(right) Paving is standard New York Parks Department material: hexagonal asphalt pavers. A band of purple-colored asphalt reiterates the forms of the meandering benches.

(below) The Javits Plaza is context-bound: it
depends on the juxtaposition of existing and new
elements to convey its meaning.

(bottom) Perspective drawing of plaza.

Schwartz makes use of the Thomas Payne Park across the street—a traditional park in its imagery, its use of plant material, and program—to activate this play of ruptures and continuities. She takes advantage of the raised condition of the site to visually appropriate the vegetation of the neighboring park into the space of the plaza. This is especially evident from a sitting position, where the top rails of the benches eliminate the middle ground, occupied by the street, between the plaza and the park. Schwartz relinquishes a boundary for her space in order to include the adjacent space. But this is only a partial acceptance. For while it aids Schwartz in achieving a desired sense of green in the plaza, it also serves her broader critique of traditional concepts of urban space. She brings the traditional park physically close in order to demonstrate her conceptual distance from it.

The strategy that leads to the functional inversion of landscape elements is the transformation of program so that it becomes the sole content of the plaza. Each element in the space is pulled out of its expected context, isolated, and dispossessed of its typical function. This alters the contribution that each element makes to the space as a whole, provoking conceptual shifts that transform relations between the elements, and between the elements and their context.

Thus benches, normally self-contained objects of finite dimension, are here stretched to meander through the site. Although still for sitting, they become the main space-forming element, articulating and layering, through their overlapping curves, the otherwise barren site. Grass, normally describing ground, is here made to blister from the pavement to form mounds that interrupt and redirect vision. In its transformed condition of non-surface, it is not conceived of as a place to walk or sit on. The mounds also contribute to the sense of green at eye level, something typically achieved with the foliage of trees or shrubs. The Central Park luminaires, normally casting light locally, are here elongated to announce the plaza from a distance.

View of the Javits Plaza as *parterre de broderie,* from one of the top floors of the Federal Building.

Schwartz has commented that her solution for the Javits Plaza is a *parterre de broderie*. This makes sense only from a stationary position in one of the top floors of the building. From the ground, though, the parterre has also been refunctionalized and, instead of lying flat on the ground to articulate and decorate it, is made into a three-dimensional space. As a result, the experience of walking in this space is closer to a picturesque English garden than to a formal French one: its ground plane is left uncompartmentalized, its fluid quality reinforced by the purple band of pavement that follows the outline of the benches. The mounds and the light poles add depth to the space through layering, rather than through the use of one point perspective. Every element in the plaza is made to function spatially in unexpected ways.

While the strategy of augmenting the scale of a familiar object may recall sculptural works, such as those of Claes Oldenburgh, that serve to monumentalize the quotidian without engaging their context, Schwartz's Javits Plaza supports its environment in multiple ways. It is engaged to it programmatically and physically—through strategies of juxtaposition and inversion—and culturally, as a critique of traditional urban space. It reveals aspects of its context as it presents itself to the visitor, demonstrating that the new, inserted, space is dependent on the old.

The bench refers to the ubiquitous New York Parks Department bench. Schwartz transforms this prototype by changing its form and color, and by expanding its program from merely to provide for sitting to layering and articulating space.

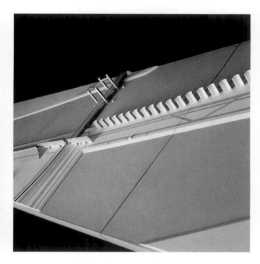

INFRASTRUCTURE

Infrastructure is an operation that combines different kinds of spaces and activities—a park, a road, a building—within its domain and is able to sustain program beyond its own logistical requirements. As an operation it works strategically to create conditions for future events, as opposed to a conventional understanding of infrastructure as an artifact that exists for the sake of a technical program. It is through this combinatorial role that the operation of infrastructure has the potential to mediate between architecture and landscape in order to contribute to the reconceptualization of the urban realm.

Early infrastructural systems that established connections were landscape corridors that traversed regions: topography such as rivers and ridges defined trade routes and road patterns. Railways, highways, and pipelines for numerous services were added to these networks of natural corridors, creating their own new cartographies. Like the natural corridors they emerged from, these infrastructures became ordering places, as well as links, around which cities and towns were organized and grew. In this capacity, infrastructure becomes a substitute for natural systems particularly in relation to larger territories, artificial systems, and points of connection.

Infrastructure facilitates connections between things that are not necessarily compatible. It usually involves a strategy, or condition, of grafting. Just as grafts leave seams that remain evident, operations of infrastructure do not result in seamless surfaces. Its seams reveal the presence of the operation by allowing different elements to come together and at the same time retain their separate identities. They are places that generate hybrid structures. Infrastructure can be significant in urban terms because of its capacity to reveal unsuspected kinship between elements long known, but assumed to be incompatible with one another, such as a park or public square with a highway.

Infrastructure as an operation diminishes the over-rationality associated with typical infrastructure projects. One strategy common to the projects presented here is the acknowledgment of site in order to provide a connection to a previously ignored physical context. Both the Allegheny Riverfront Park and the tunnel-footbridge at Lancy provide this kind of reconnection to a place. The introduction of additional program, whether functional, artistic, or phenomenological, also displaces the expected predominance of the

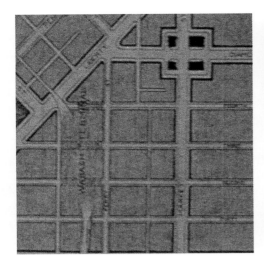

technological aspects of infrastructure, and reveals the inherent flexibility of the operation to include multiple agendas, authors, and unforeseen events. An example of an infrastructure operation that privileges the artistic over the technological is the wind screen in Rotterdam. Here, Maarten Struijs introduces an artistic agenda that blurs the distinction between environmental art and the technical requisites of wind control.

The operation of infrastructure disrupts the opposition between culture and nature, which posits landscape as an unbuilt, original condition upon which architecture, as part of culture, is built. The projects in this section provide examples of infrastructure as a built ground onto which a landscape—nature—is built. These built landscapes are not nostalgic: they do not refer to a lost nature. They acquire the spatial and functional characteristics of the places onto which they are grafted. These landscapes emerge as frameworks for urban development, as structural tissue that activates connections and supports multiple programs, and as territorries that are indistinguishable from the city. The ramps and paths in the Allegheny Riverfront Park, for example, appropriate the adjacent highway's scale and postindustrial language, taking on its program of connectivity, to join other threads of movement in the expansion of a major corridor into the city.

Infrastructure goes beyond making connections to establish communication between elements. Rather than segregating activities, it intertwines them. For instance, the Plaça de les Glories Catalanes becomes one of several centers in Barcelona, supporting and activating a large neighborhood, as well giving identity to a major highway that enters and exits the city. The tunnel-footbridge at Lancy engages the visitor to the park at several scales, providing mechanisms for self-location and inscription in a landscape that has lost all particularity. Each of these infrastructures not only organizes fundamental necessities of life, it relates this organization to cultural frameworks.

TUNNEL-FOOTBRIDGE

Lancy, Switzerland
1985–1988
Georges Descombes, Architect

The renovation of an existing park on the outskirts of Geneva presented the problem of linking it with housing across a recently widened, heavily trafficked road, as well as spanning a small brook running beneath the road. Descombes' hybrid solution of a tunnel beneath the road and a footbridge over the brook became the basis for a pedestrian infrastructure that is closely tied to the ecology and topography of the historical landscape. The paradoxical identity of this infrastructure, that is simultaneously detached from and integrated into its context, provides a distance from which to re-perceive the site, and provides at the same time an intimate reconnection that challenges the "over-rationality of the place."

According to Descombes, the successive negation of relationships between architectural artifacts and the morphology of their context began in the site in the 1920s, with the conversion of this previously rural area of groves, brooks, marshes, and winding lanes, to an industrialized market-gardening region. A rationalized, rectilinear geometry replaced the fragmented plot structure that bore traces of accumulated historical identities. Massive drainage, leveling, and sanitation of the land buried water in concrete pipes and erased topographic variation. Unconsidered development since the 1950s exacerbated the situation left by this earlier erasure of the preexisting landscape.

The architect's objective was to overturn the negation of the place by reconnecting this incomprehensible fragment of territory with temporal and spatial contexts. His interventions expose forces acting in the landscape by mapping long-erased cartographies, such as the buried brook. Like the three groupings of objects that Descombes designed within the park itself, the tunnel-footbridge identifies and measures a territory by recalling traces of its formation.

Photocollage aerial view

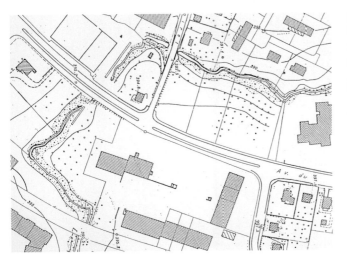

(above) Aerial view of tunnel-footbridge and heterogeneous suburban context of small detached houses, high-rise housing blocks, and sports facilities.

(left) Plan of existing conditions, 1980.

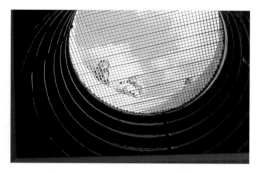

The role of the tunnel-footbridge is not only to enable movement across obstacles. It also provides a mechanism for self-location in a context where pedestrians have not been considered. It is the construction of this possibility for self-location that enables the place to become public, by allowing individuals to reappropriate it. By being positioned within it, visitors are able to map this landscape themselves, rather than having to accept it without question.

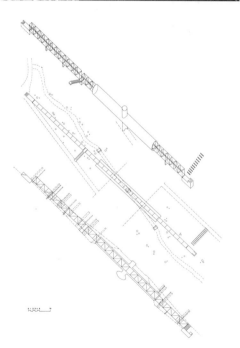

(top) Looking up through the skylight at the center of the tunnel.

(middle) Steps to footbridge near tunnel entrance: the 300-foot-long (91.4-meter-long) bridge is constructed as a wood and chain-link truss with a rough wooden board floor that runs inside the steel tube.

(above) Axonometric, plan, and section of tunnel-footbridge.

(right) Looking toward tunnel-footbridge with car on road above.

Descombes' assemblage of infrastructure objects injects a slightly disturbing presence into the landscape, causing an experiential shock that jolts the ordinariness of its context. The architect intended this feeling of strangeness to create a susceptibility within the individual to the revelation of now-invisible forces. That the project's logic exceeds its functionality is evident in the provision of a 300-foot-long (91.4-meter-long) bridge to cross what is now a 3-foot-wide (1-meter-wide) stream. The surreal absurdity of this relationship displaces emphasis away from the site's present-day realities.

Everything about the project, from the length of the footbridge to the tunnel's diameter, is intentionally too large. This scalar exaggeration stimulates an awareness of scale as an overlooked attribute of the contemporary suburban landscape. It also suggests an association with the sublime, wherein aesthetic feeling comes from the contradiction between the totality of a thing and the perceived impossibility of understanding it.

(left) Looking in tunnel, with culvert skylight above.

(right) Stair access to footbridge.

Descombes has also described the overscaling of elements as part of an attempt to join irreconcilable past and present moments in the landscape. The moments he refers to are personal: his attempt has been to plot the differences between child and adult bodies, by "stretching" his own revisited memory of being a child here, sneaking inside a culvert, or following a brook as it disappears under a road. The tunnel-footbridge has the aura of an abandoned artifact reappropriated for an unplanned use. Beginning and ending on uneven, weedy ground, it suggests a children's game, whose objective is to construct an alternative cartography, away from established routes.

(top) Looking from above to the tunnel emerging from the woods.

(above) View alongside footbridge.

Strategies that recall eighteenth-century picturesque gardens help to orchestrate passage through this late-twentieth-century suburban hybrid landscape. The reliance on associative processes of memory to organize and establish nonhierarchical relationships between elements allows these elements to remain discrete, in spite of their proximity. The skylight also recalls the picturesque device of the ruin, as if it were a caved-in fragment of antiquity. The project's modest materials and construction techniques denote a realism that belies this romantic identity. Yet this modesty also underscores the sense of operating in a "minor mode," outside official circuits. The architectural manipulation of these multiple threads creates an ambiguous place that is both "earthy and airy, hiding place and observatory" (Tironi, 1988).

(top) Detail at meeting of the footbridge and tunnel.

(middle) Detail of the bridge emerging from the tunnel.

(above) Detail of the culvert emerging from the ground.

(left) Construction view from inside the tunnel.

WIND SCREEN

Rotterdam, the Netherlands
1983–1985
Maarten Struijs, Architect, Public Works Rotterdam

The Wind Screen is a system of freestanding concrete slabs and earthen dikes that enables navigation on the Caland Canal in the harbor of Rotterdam's Brittanniehaven. Part engineering, part sculpture, part landscape, it prompts an interpretation of infrastructure as an operation that is inclusive of what are usually opposing cultures and disciplines. The wind screen derives its ambiguous identity from its relationship to the landscape: it is both detached from and integrated into its context; it is over-rationalized without losing its visual relationship to the site; it is scientifically determined without being devoid of an artistic program. The simultaneous presence of these characteristics breaks down the autonomy of the environmental barrier as technological artifact.

The Caland Canal serves to transport container shipments from the outer sea into the port of Rotterdam. The long and narrow site borders the canal on its western, windward, side. A bridge for rail and automobile traffic stands perpendicular to the site at its midpoint. South of the bridge, the site is a narrow spit of land containing mostly access roads to piers along the shore; north of the bridge, the site forms the edge of a field of oil storage tanks protected from the surrounding waterways by dikes along its perimeter. The high winds on the site exert a lateral force on the ships that can cause them to crash against the vertical supports of the bridge.

Wind tunnel research for this site had previously established an optimum height of 81 feet (25 meters) for the wind screen and a permeability of 25% to reduce the wind pressure at the navigation line. Typically, wind screens adopt the "sieve model," a continuous wall with a perforated surface that slows the wind. Struijs, while retaining the height requirement, reinterprets the sieve model in order to adopt an artistic program, and to expand the range of possibilities for the design of the barrier.

Aerial view looking north of Caland Canal. The site is the western edge of the canal.

(above) Aerial view of Caland Canal looking east,
on the windward side of the wind screen.

(below) Site plan

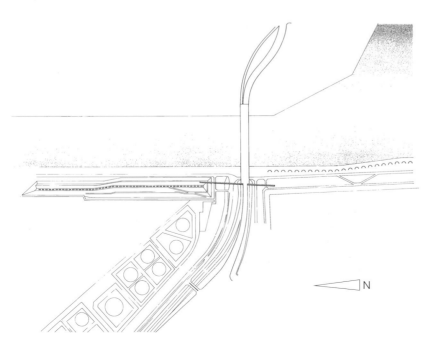

N

Detail of the concrete shell, showing
reinforced bar.

The screen is composed of freestanding concrete slabs that change configuration to form three distinct segments. South of the bridge, the wind screen takes the form of 80-foot-high (25-meter-high) semicircular shells, 29 feet (9 meters) in diameter, spaced 39 feet (12 meters) apart. At the bridge itself, the wind screen changes to slim, pier-like semi-circular shells, 6.5 feet (2 meters) in diameter, placed 4 feet (1.3 meters) apart. North of the bridge, the slabs are combined with a windbreaking earth dike: 33-foot-by-33-foot (10-meter-by-10-meter) concrete slabs rest on top of a grass embankment 49 feet (15 meters) high.

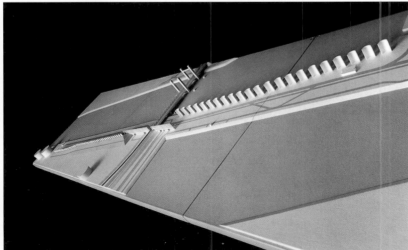

(above left) Concave shells from access road.

(left) Model, showing the three sections of the wind screen.

Struijs breaks down the typical wall-like expression of wind barriers into fragments, manipulating their spacing and proportions to reassert their individuality as free-standing sculptural pieces. Furthermore, the three segments are not aligned with each other and overlap, emphasizing the autonomy of each section and the inclusion of aesthetic, non-technical criteria informing the design.

The various configurations of the concrete slabs relate each section of the monumental structure to its context through either mimesis or function. The semicircular shells sit on the flat ground like the oil storage tanks in the surrounding landscape, visually integrating the wind screen with its industrial context. The pierlike shells in the middle section rest over a beam and do not reach the ground, allowing traffic to circulate through and around the foot of the bridge. The grass embankment to the north, appropriates the sectional profile of the adjacent dikes, changing its direction slightly in its northernmost end to join an existing dike and, in effect, to form the enclosure that protects the field from flooding. Thus, while the wind screen retains a consistent height along its length, each section changes to serve additional, unrelated, program and to express the changing conditions of the site along its 1-mile (1700-meter) length. Paradoxically, by expanding its agenda and pursuing a will to form, the architect creates a wind screen that seems to resist its own program.

(left) Looking south at the overlap between the flat concrete slabs on the dike and the pierlike concrete slabs.

(right) Looking west at the semi-circular shells from the Caland Canal.

(top right) Detail of the dike and the square slabs.

Minimalism is present in the screen's austere language, in the use of repetition, in the absence of hierarchy, and in the unsentimental, industrialized quality of the slabs. As is the case with minimalist sculpture, the gaps between the elements are as important as the elements themselves. In this project, the gaps acquire special significance. In addition to breaking down the impact of the structure on the environment, they announce that the wind screen is also about the passage, and not just the obstruction, of wind.

PLAÇA DE LES GLORIES CATALANES

Barcelona, Spain
1992
Andreu Arriola, Architect

The Plaça de les Glories Catalanes emerged first in 1859 in Idelfonso Cerda's plan for the expansion of Barcelona, and again in León Jaussely's plan of 1904. It was to be a pivotal space at the eastern section of the Diagonal, the 6.2-mile (10-kilometer) avenue that cuts diagonally across the plane of Barcelona, descending from an altitude of 328 feet (100 meters) at its western end, to sea level at its eastern end. In both proposals ,the plaza was envisioned as a strategy to relocate the center of the city to the east. However, it was never realized, and neither the relocation of the city hall nor the extensions of infrastructure such as water and sewer systems took place. As part of the decentralization and urban renewal of Barcelona during the last fifteen years, the Plaça de les Glories Catalanes was reconsidered. Its primary purpose was to support the completion of the Diagonal toward the sea, providing the basis for the construction of housing in the center of the city. In addition, located at the intersection of three of the city's main avenues—the Meridiana, the Diagonal, and the Gran Via—it would provide connections between multiple urban sectors and the highway that enters and exits the city. As a public space, the plaza has a dual role: that of providing connections to other places and at the same time supporting the establishment of neighborhoods for which it becomes a center. It serves to disperse and combine at the same time.

Pedestrian and automobile entrances to the plaza.

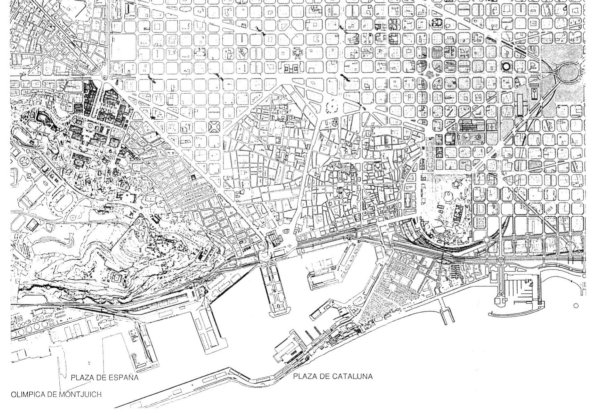

(above) Aerial view

(left) Context plan, with project at upper right.

PLAZA DE ESPAÑA

OLIMPICA DE MONTJUICH

PLAZA DE CATALUNA

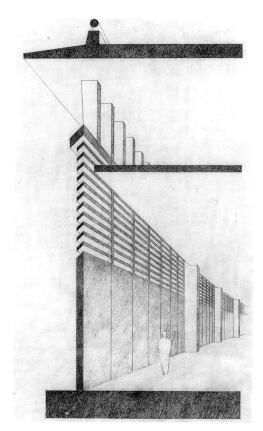

Like the majority of open space available in the postindustrial city, the plaça had become marginalized as a result of uncoordinated urban development. Its center, although vegetated, was an empty, unvalued area that testified to a clash of urban geometries. Arriola overturned this amorphous condition, transforming the site from wasteland to constructed nature, and from margin to center. They did not, however, attempt a recovery of the original status of the landscape. Instead, they construed landscape as a series of evolutionary events producing an environment that does not segregate urban functions, e.g., transportation versus civic space. The project produces a new centrality based on the superimposition of different uses, creating spaces that are inclusive of landscape architecture, urbanism, and architecture.

(above left) Section perspective showing parking-structure wall and highway above.

(above) Model

(left and below) Views from the street level of the highway as it joins the parking building.

(bottom) Site prior to intervention. By the 1980s, the site had evolved from an intersection of three avenues to a chaotic knot of viaducts, elevated pedestrian walkways, and a railroad.

(below) Elevation from the street.

(bottom) View from exit ramp in the interior of the circle.

The material for the project is traffic itself: vehicular circulation at different speeds—the geometry of motion—fixes the scale and dimensions of the elements (Arriola, 1993). Two superimposed oval rings separate local traffic from through traffic. The upper ring is for high-speed traffic in and out of town. The lower ring is for local traffic and pedestrian circulation. The vertical space between the two tiers of traffic is conceptualized as a building. Its outer (street) and inner (park) façades define the edges of the plaza. The strong figural presence of the circle in the urban fabric, a form that recalls an ancient civic structure—colosseum or amphitheater—contradicts its porosity. The building walls are perforated by multiple walks and vehicular openings that make the ground plane of the city continuous again, reestablishing connections between sidewalks and local streets, organizing and supporting life in the surrounding neighborhood. The choice of a parking garage as program for the building is also meaningful as a structure of connection between neighborhood, highway, and city.

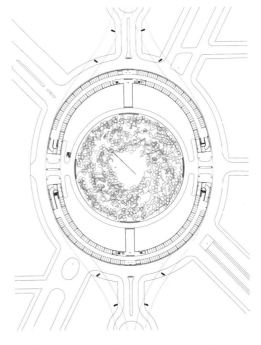

(above) Site plan showing plan of parking structure.

(left) Site plan showing park.

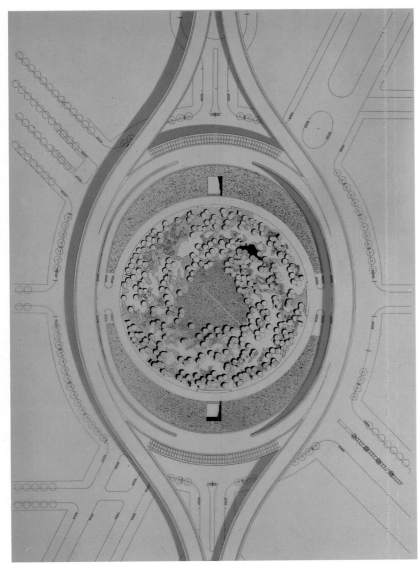

The combinatorial function of the operation becomes especially evident in the interior of the circle, where an urban park, commemorative stone slabs, vehicular ramps, and light beams that activate the space at night for the passing cars, all coexist within its space.

(top) View from exit ramp.

(above) The park at night. The functions of the park are not exclusively for the pedestrian: at night, beams of light emanate upward from the tablets to activate an experience of the place for the automobile in motion.

(left) Stone tablets that commemorate historical events in Catalonia.

The Plaça de les Glories Catalanes is infrastructure in that it supports the development of an entire urban sector as well as the organization of life at a localized scale. It presents a comprehensive reflection on the contemporary city as a system that is implicated in facilitating connections as much as social processes. The proximity of activities that result from mixing programs—highway, building, public park, commemoration—eliminate the frontiers between them, enabling new interpretations of infrastructure.

(top) Interior view of parking building.

(above) Context photomontage showing the proposal for the Plaça de les Glories Catalanes, with other future development in the area.

ALLEGHENY RIVERFRONT PARK

Pittsburgh, Pennsylvania, USA
1995–1998
Michael Van Valkenburgh Associates, Inc., Landscape Architects
Ann Hamilton and Michael Mercil, Artists

This project is a two-tiered park that has been tightly fit between existing infrastructures: the Allegheny River, the Tenth Street bypass (a four lane highway) and Fort Duquesne Boulevard. The design does not attempt to establish differences between the park and the infrastructure adjacent to it. It resists traditional dichotomies of city-versus-nature and built-versus-natural, instead presenting the park as a graft that acquires aspects of its host structures, the river and the highway. This inclusive strategy is emblematic of the operation of infrastructure, where both nature and city are understood as original conditions of the landscape. It also reveals infrastructure as an operation that is implicated in constructing relations between the organization of production, and cultural frameworks of the aesthetic, the social, and the personal. Conceived as two additional strands in the infrastructure corridor, the park activates larger connections between the city and the region. It functions as a pedestrian corridor, a connector to regional bike paths, and a local neighborhood park. As with the development of a traditional transportation infrastructure, these larger-scale issues have generated the conception of the park.

(above) Historical map of Pittsburgh. The Allegheny Riverfront Park connects Point State Park, now existing almost in isolation, to regional bike paths, by providing a continuous strip of parkland along the north side of the city.

(right) Section through Allegheny Riverfront Park, both levels.

(below right) Site plan

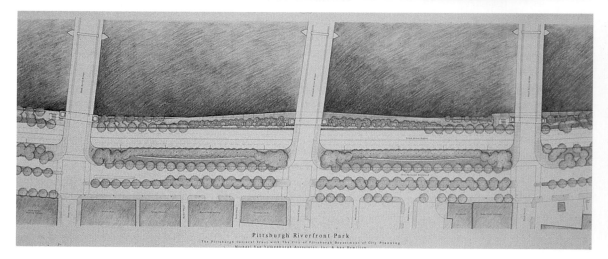

View of the lower park from the bridge. Red maple (*Acer rubrum*), redbud (*Cercis canadensis*) sycamore (*Platanus occidentalis*), silver maple (*Acer saccharinum*), and cottonwood (*Populus deltoides*) are planted in groves amid boulders, capturing the imagery of volunteer plants colonizing the edge.

(top) Section, lower park showing cantilevered
concrete walk.

(above) Perspective, lower park.

Van Valkenburgh's objective was to reintroduce the unpredictable and the unstable to the river's edge—presently paved over for parking—by exposing the site to the freeze-thaw cycles and erosive processes of the river. The plantings' precarious location at the very edge of the site reveals an expectation of impermanence that would support continual transformation in the park. The concrete walk that meanders amidst the plantings aquires an infrastructural identity as it cantilevers over the water to overcome the narrow 20-foot (6.1-meter) width of the site. The park's suggestion of ruin, created by the juxtaposition of this artifact-walk with the seemingly uncomposed and unaestheticized planting, refers to the region's immediate, post-industrial past—evident in the nearby abandoned steel mills that are slowly being assailed by indigenous vegetation.

The concrete walk meanders around the boulder fields connecting the Sixth, Seventh, and Ninth Street bridges.

The upper park is separated from the lower by a 30-foot (9.1-meter) change in grade and a four-lane highway. A pedestrian promenade that extends from Tenth Street to the tip of the city at Point State Park, its main event is a continuous bench that describes the dipping topography of the site. Maintaining a constant top elevation, the base follows the contour of the terrain, making the bench vary in height from a 6-inch (15-centimeter) curb to a 20-inch (51-centimeter) sitting wall. The bench joins the landscape to the city by describing the particularities of the local topography through the conventions of the urban artifact. At the upper park, the tree species, London Plane Tree (*Platanus x acerifolia*) and Pagoda tree (*Sophora japonica*), are traditional trees in the American city, reflecting the more stable and predictable urban environment where they exist. In this project, Van Valkenburgh presents a landscape that oscillates between a condition of riparian corridor, with moments of hyperintensified, unstable, raw nature, and urbane, aesthetically considered pedestrian promenade.

View of Upper Park Sloped Lawn and Seating Edge

Pedestrian ramps at the intersection of the Seventh Street bridge connect the two levels of the park. In these hybrid structures—connectors, sound blocks, and vegetal backdrops—the park as graft becomes most evident. The ramps appropriate the language of infrastructure. Their extraordinary 270-foot (82.3-meter) length is more typical of a highway than of traditional pedestrian paths. Their elevation also reveals a desire to identify them with highway rather than with park. Their supporting structures are solid, continuous concrete walls that appear, from across the river, like vehicular ramps. This assimilation of pieces of the park into its infrastructural context points to the necessary artifice of landscapes in the contemporary city, by suggesting the possibility of infrastructure as original ground of the contemporary urban landscape.

(top) Looking down the pedestrian ramp. The subject is inscribed in the figural prominence given to the ramps and walks throughout the park, and in the detailing of the bronze handrails on the ramps. Their undulating rhythms pace the body as it ascends or descends through space.

(above) Pedestrian ramp and the lower park. The lower park is a sliver of land at water level between the river and the Tenth Street bypass.

(left) Perspective drawing of upper park.

Detail, concrete walk, with shadows from the
handrail cast on its surface.

Finally, the multiple activities envisioned to take place in the park present infrastructure as a public domain that activates relations at multiple scales, promoting social relations within its space, in addition to its more traditional functions of facilitating connections to larger regions.

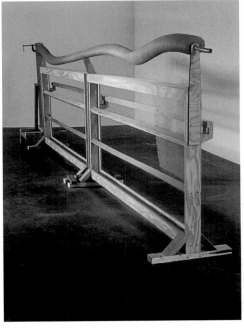

(above) Unlike most infrastructure projects, where the machine is inscribed in the work to the exclusion of everything else, the Allegheny Riverfront Park also inscribes and locates landscape processes. Reeds collected from the river were embedded in the concrete to reference erosive processes at the river's edge.

(top right) Detail, finished concrete walk.

(bottom right) Study model for bronze handrail, Ann Hamilton and Michael Mercil, artists.

References

Operations between architecture and landscape

Homi K. Bhabha, "DissemiNation," *Nation and Narration*, H. K. Bhabha, ed., London: Routledge, 1990, p. 314.
Rosalind Krauss and Yves-Alain Bois, *Formless: a User's Guide*, New York: Zone Books, 1997, p. 15.
Lauren Sedoksky, "Down and Dirty: L'informe at the Centre Georges Pompidou" in *Art Forum*, Summer 1996, p. 90.
Jane Flax, "Something Is Happening: On Writing in a Transitional State," *Thinking Fragments*, Berkeley, 1990.
The Once and Future Park, edited by Herbert Muschamp, Diana Balmori, Patricia Philips et al. (1993).
John Dixon Hunt, *Gardens and the Picturesque*: Studies in the History of Landscape Architecture, Cambridge, MA: MIT Press. 1992, p. 289.

Querini Stampalia Foundation

Maria Antonietta Crippa, Carlo Scarpa, *il Pensiero il Disegno i Progetti*, Milan: Jaca Book, 1984.
Sergio Los, *Carlo Scarpa*, Cologne, Taschen, 1993.
Richard Murphy, *Querini Stampalia Foundation: Carlo Scarpa*, London: Phaidon Press, 1993.

Loyola Law School

Carol Burns, "The Gehry Phenomenon," *Thinking the Present: Recent American Architecture*, K. Michael Hays and Carol Burns, eds., New York: Princeton Architectural Press, 1990, pp. 72–88.
Germano Celant, "Reflections on Frank Gehry," *Frank Gehry Buildings and Projects*, Arnell and Bickford, eds., New York: Rizzoli, 1985, pp. 5–15.
Sandro Marpillero, "Gehry in Sequence: A Glance in the Kitchen," *Casabella* 581, July–August, 1991, pp. 27–28.

Villa Dall' Ava

Isabelle Auricoste, "On Yves Brunier's Work," *Pages Paysages*, No. 4, 1992/93, pp. 98–99.
O.M.A. Rem Koolhaas, and Bruce Mau, *S. M. L. XL*. New York: The Monacelli Press, 1995, pp. 130–193.
Bart Lootsma, "Rem Koolhaas/OMA: Wall of Frustration," *Daidalos: Magic of Materials II*, August 1995, pp. 74–83.
Andrew Davis, "Interview with Rem Koolhaas at the Villa Dall' Ava," Harvard Graduate School of Design student project, 1996.
Alejandro Zaera, "Notes for a Topographic Survey," and "Villa Dall' Ava," *El Croquis, Rem Koolhaas–O.M.A. 1987–1992*, 1992, pp. 32–52. 136–157.

School at Morella

Peter Buchanan, "Provocative and Participatory Places. Enric Miralles and Carmen Pinós," *Architectural Review*, No. 1121, July 1990, pp. 74–87.
William J. R. Curtis, "Mental Maps and Social Landscapes: The Architecture of Miralles and Pinós," *El Croquis*, June–September 1991, pp. 6–20.
Lauren Kogod, "A Commentary on the Work of Enric Miralles and Carmen Pinós", *Assemblage 7*, 1988, pp. 108–111.
Kogod, "New Geographies, Boarding School," *Architecture + Urbanism* 51–52, January–April 1995, pp. 188–191.
Anne Marshall, ed., *Carmé Pinós*, Urbana: Univ. of Illinois, 1995.

Barnes Residence

Brian Carter, ed., *Patkau Architects*, Halifax: Tunis Press, 1994.
Thomas Fisher, "Design as a Form of Inquiry," *Progressive Architecture*, September 1995, pp. 53–60.
John McMinn, "Barnes House, Nanaimo B.C.," *Canadian Architect*, Vol. 41, No. 2, Feb. 1996, pp. 22–26.

Brion Cemetery

Kenneth Frampton, "Carlo Scarpa and the Adoration of the Joint," *Studies in Tectonic Culture: The Poetics of Construction in Nineteenth and Twentieth Century Architecture*, Cambridge: MIT Press, 1995, pp. 299–326.
Andrea Kahn, "Disclosure: Approaching Architecture," *Harvard Architecture Review*, 8, 1992, pp. 16–18.
Pierluigi Nicolin, "His most important work. Carlo Scarpa; the Brion cemetery-tomb at San Vito di Altivole," *Lotus International*, 38, 1983, p. 45.

Stone House

Theodora Vischer, "Interview," *Herzog & De Meuron: Projects and Buildings*, Wilfried Wang, ed., New York: Rizzoli, 1990, pp. 7-15
Alejandro Zaera, "Continuities: Interview with Herzog & De Meuron," *El Croquis*, 60, 199, pp. 6-23.
Alejandro Zaera, "Herzog & De Meuron: Between the Face and the Landscape," *El Croquis*, 60, 1993, pp. 24-36.

Bamboo Garden

Architecture d'Aujourd'Hui (theme issue on Chemetoff), February 1996, No. 303, pp. 60-73.
Isabelle Auricoste, et al., *Parc-Ville Villette*, Paris: Champ Vallon, 1987.
"Jardin des Bambous. Paris 1987," *Techniques et Architecture* , No. 403, August-September 1992, pp. 46-49.
"Le Jardin des Bambous/Parc de la Villette," *Architecture d'Aujourd'Hui*, April 1989, No. 262, pp. 44-47.
"Les Jardins de la Villette," *Architecture d'Aujourd'Hui*, December 1981, No. 218, pp. 32-33.

Cemetery at Igualada

Peter Buchanan, "Enric Miralles & Carmen Pinós," *Architectural Review*, May 1986, pp. 80-83.
Lauren Kogod, "A Commentary on the Work of Enric Miralles and Carmen Pinós," *Assemblage* 7, October 1988, pp. 108-111.
Enric Miralles, "From what time is this place?," *Topos* 8, September 1994, pp. 102-108.
Frank Werner, "Locations of Physical Sensation. On Two Works by Carmen Pinós and Enric Miralles," *Daidalos*, September 15, 1992, pp. 110-116.
Anatxu Zabalbeascoa, *Igualada Cemetery, Architecture in Detail*, London: Phaidon, 1996.

Thomson Factory

Christine Dalnoky and Michel Desvigne, "Layout of Landscaping and Grounds, Thomson Factory Saint-Quentin-en-Yvelines, design 1991-execution 1992," *The Landscape: Four International Landscape Designers*, 1995, pp. 182-187.
Christine Dalnoky and Michel Desvigne, "Clearing the Way for Architecture," *Pages Paysages*, No. 4, 92/93, pp. 66-71.
Dorothée Imbert, "Of Site and Time," *The Landscape: Four International Landscape Designers*, 1995, pp. 53-75.

Kimbell Art Museum

Michael Benedikt, *Deconstructing the Kimbell: An Essay on Meaning in Architecture*, New York: Sites Books, 1991.
Michael Brawne, *Kimbell Art Museum: Louis Kahn*, London: Phaidon, 1992.
Patricia C. Loud, *The Art Museums of Louis I. Khan*, Durham: Duke University Press, 1989.
Patricia C. Loud, "History of the Kimbell Art Museum," *In Pursuit of Quality*, The Kimbell Art Museum, New York, 1987.

Municipal Ocean Swimming Pool

Kenneth Frampton, "Poesis and Transformation: The Architecture of Alvaro Siza," *El Croquis*, 68-69, 1994, pp.10-24.
José Paulo dos Santos, ed., *Alvaro Siza: Works & Projects 1954-1992*. Barcelona: Editorial Gustavo Gili, S.A., 1993, pp. 86-93.

Haarlemmer Houttuinen Housing

Peter Buchanan, "The New Amsterdam School," *Architectural Review*, January 1985, pp. 14-38.
Herman Hertzberger, "Haarlemmer Houtinnen/Amsterdam, The Netherlands/1978-1982," *Mies Van Der Rohe Award for European Architecture 1990*, pp. 66-69.
Herman Hertzberger, "Recent works of Herman Hertzberger," *Architecture + Urbanism*, 12 (159), December 1983, pp. 39-74.
Herman Hertzberger, *"The Street," Lessons for Students in Architecture*, Rotterdam: Uitgeverij, pp. 48-63.

Villa Cecilia

R. Levine, "Jardines Villa Cecilia," *El Croquis: Spanish Contemporary Architecture 1975–1990*, 1990, pp. 292–299.
Jean Francois Pousse, "Jardin de la Villa Cecilia, Barcelona," *Techniques & Architecture*, 383, May 1989, pp. 112–115.

Etienne Dolet Public Housing

Catherine Mosbach, "More Than Pictures: Two Projects from Paris," *Topos*, 12, September 1995, pp. 17–23.

Insertion

Joan Busquets, "Scales of Activity," *Rassegna*, 37, March 1989, Joan Busquets, ed., V. Gregotti, ed. (series), pp. 38–53.

Plaça del General Moragues

Peter Buchanan, "Barcelona Park & Plaza," *Architectural Review*, September 1989, pp. 81–84.
Peter Buchanan, "Regenerating Barcelona with Parks and Plazas," *Architectural Review*, June 1984, pp. 33–46.

Fossar de les Moreres

Andreu Arriola, "Building the City Out of Empty Spaces," *Modern Park Design: Recent Trends*, Andreu Arriola, Adriaan Geuze, Steen Høyer, Bernard Huet, Peter Latz, David Louwerse, Norfried Pohl, and Clemens Steenbergen, eds., Amsterdam: THOTH Publishers, 1993, pp. 56–65.

Two-Way Mirror Cylinder Inside Cube and Video Café

Alain Charre, Marie-Paule MacDonald, and Marc Perelman, *Dan Graham*, Paris: Éditions Dis Voir, 1995.
Alfonso Pérez-Méndez, "Glass Garden: A Rooftop Pavilion at Dia," *SITES*, 25, 1993, pp. 28–39.

Tunnel-Footbridge

Kenneth Frampton, "En busca del Paisaje Moderno=In search of the Modern Landscape," *Arquitectura*, 1990 July–August, v. 72, No. 285, pp. 52–73.
Giordano Tironi, ed., *Georges Descombes: Shifting Sites*, Rome: Gangemi editore, 1988; with essays by Franco Purini, André Corboz, Herman Hertzberger, Descombes, and others.

Wind Screen

Enrico Morteo, "Barriere contro il vento, Rotterdam," *Domus*, 737, April 1992, pp.102–108.
Wolfgang J. Stock, "Wind Baffle at a Rotterdam Canal," *Topos*, 10, March 1995, pp. 22–27.
Marteen Struijs and Joop Schilperoord, "The Wind Barrier along the Caland Canal near Rotterdam," *Report of the IABSE Symposium*, Versailles 1987, pp. 615–620.
Marteen Struijs, "Ecran antivent dans le port de Rotterdam," *Bauen in Beton*, 1990–91, pp. 28–31.

Plaça de les Glories Catalanes

Andreu Arriola, "Building the City Out of Empty Spaces," *Modern Park Design*, Amsterdam, 1993, pp. 57–65.
Joan Busquets, "Scales of Activity," *Rassegna*, 37, March 1989, Joan Busquets, ed., V. Gregotti, ed. (series), pp. 38–53.
Alejandro Zaera, "Between Simulation and Connection. Public Space in Contemporaneity," *El Croquis*, 1989, pp. 119-132

Project Credits

Querini Stampalia Foundation

Venice, Italy
1961–1963
Carlo Scarpa, Architect
Giuseppe Mazzariol, Landscape Architect

Loyola Law School

Los Angeles, California, USA
1981–1984
Frank O. Gehry & Associates, Inc.
Project team: Frank O. Gehry, Greg Walsh,
Hak Sik Son, Rene G. Ilustre.

Villa Dall' Ava

St. Cloud, France
1984–1991
Rem Koolhaas, Office for Metropolitan Architecture
Project team: Xaveer de Geyter, Jeroen Thomas
Yves Brunier, Landscape Architect
Petra Blaisse, Interior Consultant
Mark Mimram, Engineer

School at Morella

Morella, Spain
1986–1993
Carmen Pinós & Enric Miralles, Architects
Carmen Pinós, Construction Architect
Project team: Se Duch, Juan Antonio Andreu, Rodrigo Prats

Barnes Residence

Nanaimo, British Columbia, Canada
1990-1992
Patkau Architects
Project team: Tim Newton, John Patkau,
Patricia Patkau, David Shone, Tom Robertson

Brion Cemetery

San Vito d' Altivole, Treviso, Italy
1967–1978
Carlo Scarpa, Architect
Pietro Porcinai, Landscape Architect

Stone House

Tavole, Italy
1985–1988
Jacques Herzog &
Pierre De Meuron, Architects

Bamboo Garden

Parc de la Villette, Paris, France
1986–1989
Alexandre Chemetoff, Bureau des Paysages
Project team: Alexandre Chemetoff,
Martine Renan, Daniel Buren, Bernhart Leitner, Artists
Jean Louis Cohen, Architect
Henry Bardsley, Engineer

Igualada Cemetery

Igualada, Spain
1985–1991
Enric Miralles & Carmen Pinós, Architects
Enric Miralles, Construction Architect
Project team: Josep Misa, Joan Callis,
Eva Prats, Albert Ferre, Se Duch

Thomson Factory

Landscape and parking areas
Saint-Quentin-en-Yvelines, France
1991–1992
Desvigne & Dalnoky
Project team: Michel Desvigne,
Christine Dalnoky, Bernard Rouyer
Renzo Piano, Architect

Kimbell Art Museum

West entrance
Fort Worth, Texas, USA
1966–1972
Louis Kahn, Architect
George Patton, Landscape Architect

Municipal Ocean Swimming Pool

Leça da Palmeira, Matushinos, Portugal
1961–1966
Alvaro Siza, Architect
Project team: Beatriz Madueira, Antonio Madueira

Haarlemmer Houttuinen Housing

Amsterdam, Netherlands
1978-1982
Architectuurstudio Herman Hertzberger

Villa Cecilia

Barcelona, Spain
1983-1986
Jose Antonio Martinez Lapeña & Elias Torres Tur, Architects
Francisco Lopez Hernandez, Artist
Project team: Guillermo Font, Tono Gallard, J. Ignacio Gratacos, Inma
Josemaria, Eileen Liebman, Moises Martinez, Benjamin Plegezuelos,
Marta Pujol, Thomas Rotzler, Marcos Viader, Miguel Viader

Etienne Dolet Public Housing

Outdoor spaces
Issy-les Moulineaux, France
1990-1992
Catherine Mosbach, Landscape Architect

Robert F. Wagner, Jr. Park

New York, New York, USA
1993-1996
Machado and Silvetti Associates, Inc.
Project team: Rodolfo Machado (Principal in Charge),
Jorge Silvetti, Designers. Peter Logfren,
Douglas Dolezal, Elizabeth Gibb, Nader Tehrani.
Olin Partnership, Landscape Architects
Project team: Laurie D. Olin (Principal in Charge), Lucinda Sanders,
Bobbie King, Karen Janosky.
Lynden B. Miller, Garden Designer

Plaça del General Moragues

Barcelona, Spain
1986-1988
Olga Tarrasó, Architect, City of Barcelona
Project team: S. Gassó, A. Costa, P. Aguilar

Fossar de les Moreres

Barcelona, Spain
1989
Carmen Fiol, Architect
Project team: Pere Raich, Rosa María Hugués,
Montserrat Ribas, Poli González

Two-way Mirror Cylinder Inside Cube and Video Salon

Rooftop Installation at the Dia Center for the Arts
New York, New York, USA
1991
Dan Graham, Artist
Baratloo-Balch Architects

Jacob Javits Plaza

New York, New York, USA
1995-1996
Martha Schwartz, Inc.
Project team: Martha Schwartz, Laura Rutledge,
Maria Bellalta, Chris McFarlane, Michael Blier, Leo Jew

Tunnel-Footbridge

Lancy, Switzerland
1985-1988
Georges Descombes, Architect
Project team: Jan Gebert, Alain Léveille

Wind Screen

Rotterdam, Netherlands
1983-1985
Maarten Struijs, Architect, Public Works Rotterdam
Joop Schilperood, Engineer
Frans de Witt, Artist

Plaça de les Glories Catalanes

Barcelona, Spain
1992
Andreu Arriola, Architect
Project team: J. Mas, O. Ribera. A. Monglous, Engineer

Allegheny Riverfront Park

Pittsburgh, Pennsylvania, USA
1994-1997
Michael Van Valkenburgh Associates, Inc.
Project team: Michael Van Valkenburgh,
Laura Solano, Mathew Urbansky.
Ann Hamilton and Michael Mercil, Artists

Photo Credits

Front Cover

Duccio Malagamba

Back Cover, clockwise from top left

Linda Pollak, Catherine Mosbach, Querini Stampalia Foundation, Mathew Becker

page 2

© Peter Aaron/ESTO. All rights reserved

Reciprocity Introduction, left to right, pages 14-15

Querini Stampalia Foundation, Linda Pollak, Duccio Malagamba, Michael Moran, James Dow, Querini Stampalia Foundation

Querini Stampalia Foundation, pages 16–21

Photographs courtesy of the Querini Stampalia Foundation, Venice, except as noted.
Linda Pollak: page 16
Drawings by Don Freeman

Loyola Law School, pages 22–27

© Michael Moran: page 22
Anita Berrizbeitia: pages 25 (below); 26; 27 (below)
Sandro Marpillero: page 25 (above, right)
Drawings and model photographs courtesy of Frank O. Gehry & Associates, Inc.

Villa Dall' Ava, pages 28–35

© Peter Aaron/ESTO. All rights reserved: pages 29; 33 (below)
Linda Pollak: pages 30; 31 (left); 32 (above left and right); 33; 34; 35
Drawings courtesy of OMA

School at Morella, pages 36–41

© Duccio Malagamba: pages 36; 37 (above); 39 (left); 41
© Hisao Suzuki: pages 37 (below); 39 (below)
Drawings courtesy of Carmen Pinós

Barnes House, pages 42–47

Photographs © James Dow
Drawings courtesy of Patkau Architects

Materiality Introduction, left to right, pages 48-49

Linda Pollak, Enric Miralles, Desvigne + Dalnoky, Elizabeth Meyer, Linda Pollak, Linda Pollak

Brion Cemetery, pages 50–55

Linda Pollak: pages 50; 51; 52; 53; 54 (above left and below right); 55 (above and below right)
Anita Berrizbeitia: pages 54 (above right); 55 (left)
Drawings by Angela Chieh (pages 51; 52) and courtesy of Archivio Scarpa, Trevignano, Italy

Stone House, pages 56–61

All photographs by Margherita Spiluttini
Drawings courtesy of Herzog & De Meuron

Bamboo Garden, pages 62–67

Elizabeth Meyer: pages 62; 67 (below)
Linda Pollak: pages 63; 64; 65 (above and below right); 66; 67 (above)
Kate Orff: page 65 (left)
Drawings by Laura T. Brogna

Igualada Cemetery, pages 68–75

Duccio Malagamba: pages 69; 74 (below right)
Linda Pollak: pages 68; 70 (below); 72 (above left and below right); 74 (above left) ; 75 (above left and below right)
Giovanni Zanzi: page 70 (above)
Enric Miralles: pages 71; 72 (below left)
Sandro Marpillero: page 73 (above and below)
Drawings and model photographs courtesy of Enric Miralles

Thomson Factory, pages 76–81

All drawings and photographs courtesy of Michel Desvigne

Threshold Introduction, left to right, pages 82-83

Lourdes Lansana, Hisao Suzuki, Anita Berrizbeitia, Alexandre Turbant, Herman Hertzberger, Kimbell Museum

Kimbell Art Museum, pages 84-89

Michael Bodycomb: page 85
Caroline Constant: pages 84, 87 (top right, bottom right)
Kimbell Museum: page 86 (right, below left)
Linda Pollak: pages 86 (above left); 87 (middle right, bottom); 88; 89
Drawing page 84, courtesy of the Kimbell Art Museum
Drawings page 85, courtesy of The Architectural Archives, University of Pennsylvania

Municipal Ocean Swimming Pool, pages 90-97

Hisao Suzuki ©: pages 91; 92 (above)
Matthew Becker: pages 92 (below); 93; 94; 95; 96; 97
Paul Scott: page 92 (above right)
Drawings courtesy of Alvaro Siza

Haarlemmer Houttuinen Housing, pages 98-103

Herman Hertzberger: pages 98; 99 (left); 103
Amy Lin: pages 100; 101; 102
Drawings courtesy of Herman Hertzberger

Villa Cecilia, pages 104-111

Lourdes Jansana: pages 105; 107; 109 (above)
Courtesy of Torres/Lapeña: pages 106 (above left); 107 (below right)
Linda Pollak: pages 107 (above right); 108; 109 (below); 110; 111
Drawings courtesy of Torres/Lapeña

Etienne Dolet Public Housing, pages 112-119

Alexandre Turbant: pages 113; 114; 116 (above right); 117 (below right)
Catherine Mosbach: pages 116 (above left and below right); 117; 118; 119
Drawings courtesy of Catherine Mosbach

Robert F. Wagner, Jr. Park, pages 120-125

Anita Berrizbeitia: pages 122 (top); 124; 125 (below)
Laurie Olin: pages 122 (middle, above, right); 123; 125 (above)
Drawings pages 120-121 courtesy of Olin Partnership
Drawings pages 120, 123, courtesy of Machado Silvetti Associates, Inc.

Insertion Introduction, left to right, pages 126-127

Carmen Fiol, J. Espinas, Dan Graham, Olga Tarrasó, Alan Ward, Carmen Fiol

Plaça del General Moragues, pages 128-133

Linda Pollak: pages 128; 130 (above); 131; 132; 133
J. Espinas: pages 129 (center right); 130 (below)
Drawings courtesy of Olga Tarrasó

Fossar de les Moreres, pages 134-139

Carmen Fiol: pages 134; 135; 136 (left and above right);
138 (left above and center); 139 (left)
Lluís Casals: pages 137 (right center); 138 (left below and right)
Linda Pollak: page 139
Drawings and model photographs courtesy of Carmen Fiol

Two-Way Mirror Cylinder Inside Cube, pages 140-145

Dan Graham: pages 140 (right); 142 (left above and right); 144; 145
Baratloo-Balch Architects: page 143 (below)
Drawings courtesy of Baratloo-Balch Architects

Jabob Javits Plaza, pages 146-151

© Alan Ward, pages 147, 148, 150, 151
Anita Berrizbeitia: page 149 (above)
Drawings courtesy of Martha Schwartz, Inc.

Infrastructure Introduction, left to right, pages 152-153

Michael Van Valkenburgh, George Descombes, Maarten Struijs, Michael
Van Valkenburgh, Georges Descombes, Andrev Arriola

Tunnel-Footbridge, pages 154-159

Jacques Berthet: pages 154; 156 (left center)
Georges Descombes: pages 155; 156 (left above and right);
157; 158; 159

Wind Screen, pages 160-165

© Aerocamera Michel Hofmeester: page 160
Dick Sellenraad, Aeroview b.r. Rotterdam, Holland: page 161
PAC Rook: PAC Rook Vlídingen, the Netherlands: pages 162; 164-165
Paula Mejerink: page 163 (top)
Drawing by Chen-Chen Chang
Model photograph courtesy of Maarten Struijs

Plaça de les Glories Catalanes, pages 166-173

Ferran Freixa: pages 166; 167; 172 (center)
Andreu Arriola: page 169 (botton)
Linda Pollak: pages 170; 172 (bottom); 173 (top)
Antoni Bernad: pages 169 (top, middle); 172 (above)
Drawings and model photograph courtesy of Andreu Arriola

Allegheny Riverfront Park, pages 174-181

All photographs and drawings courtesy of Michael Van Valkenburgh
Associates, Inc.

About the Authors

Anita Berrizbeitia is a landscape architect who has worked on a broad range of projects, from public spaces and campuses to residential gardens. She taught in the Department of Landscape Architecture at the Harvard Graduate School of Design from 1992–1998, and is currently Assistant Professor in the Department of Landscape Architecture and Regional Planning at the University of Pennsylvania Graduate School of Fine Arts. Her essays have been published in *Architecture + Urbanism* (A+U), *Public Art Review*, *Daniel Urban Kiley: The Early Gardens* (Princeton Architectural Press), and *Recovering Landscape* (Princeton Architectural Press).

Linda Pollak is an architect in the New York firm of Marpillero Pollak Architects and teaches in the department of architecture at the Harvard Graduate School of Design. She has received grants from the National Endowment for the Arts and the Graham Foundation for Advanced Studies in the fine arts for her research on urban outdoor spaces, parts of which are published in *Lotus International*, *Public Art Issues*, *Daidalos*, *Appendx*, and the *Harvard Design* magazine. Ms. Pollak is a winner of the Architectural League of New York's Young Architects Competition, for her own projects between architecture and landscape. Her design work has appeared in publications such as the *Designed Landscape Forum*, *House and Garden*, *Daidalos*, *Journal of Architectural Education*, *Pages Paysages*, *L'Arca*, and *Casabella*.

Authors' Contributions

There are two kinds of authorship in this book: Berrizbeitia's and Pollak's joint authorship of the essay "Operations between Architecture and Landscape" and the introductions to the five sections, and their individual authorship of the project texts. Berrizbeitia wrote about the Querini Stampalia Foundation; the School at Morella; the Barnes Residence; the Stone House; the Bamboo Garden; the Thomson Factory; the Kimbell Art Museum; Robert F. Wagner, Jr. Park; Jacob Javits Plaza; Wind Screen; Plaça de les Glories Catalanes; and Allegheny Riverfront Park. Pollak wrote about the Loyola Law School; Villa Dall'Ava; Brion Cemetery; Igualada Cemetery; the Municipal Ocean Swimming Pool; Haarlemmer Houttuinen Housing; Villa Cecilia; Etienne Dolet Public Housing; Plaça del General Moragues; Fossar de les Moreres; Two-Way Mirror Cylinder Inside Cube and Video Café; and the Tunnel-Footbridge.

Aultermann

St. Louis Community College
at Meramec
LIBRARY